The NLP Coach Companion

What to do and when to do it.

How to reveal potential
and coach performance

Neal Anderson

www.valleytraining.co.uk
14 Sunnyside, Kendal, Cumbria, LA9 7DJ

First published 2011. 2nd Edition published 2011

ISBN 978-0-9568353-3-8

CONTENTS

Exploring & Setting Goals 71

Resourceful States 85

Shifting Perspectives 107

Motivation 125

ACKNOWLEDGEMENTS

As with many works, this book represents a compendium of ideas and learnings from several years experience. I have had the pleasure to come to know many inspirational participants through training courses, research and reading. Thanks to all my previous course members for their encouragement and feedback. The book would not have been possible without the wisdom of the following thinkers, trainers and writers: John Grinder, Richard Bandler, Gregory Bateson, Virginia Satir, Robert Dilts, Wyatt Woodsmall, Steven Gilligan, John Overdurf, Julie Silverthorn, Dr Susi Strang Wood and many others.

The appendix contains a list of techniques and the primary reference from which topics in the book are based. Whilst the inspiration for the content of this book is from many sources, this presentation of thoughts and activities, including any errors or omissions, is my own design. Sincere apologies if any copyright is not fully acknowledged – please email me at neal@valleytraining.co.uk with any amendments.

Ben Dowman, my co-director at Sugar NLP has been invaluable in providing insight, a sounding board and perspective for my thoughts, whims and interpretations. Thank you.

Finally, thanks to my son Sam and Tryfan my golden retriever for keeping me connected to here and now experiences. Most importantly thank you to Kelly my beautiful wife for encouraging and supporting me.

INTERNATIONAL NLP TRAINERS ASSOCIATION

The content of this book supports the Coach Practitioner syllabus of The International NLP Trainers Association.

FOREWORDS

It is my pleasure to recommend to you this powerful and much needed book on Coaching by my student Neal Anderson.

NLP is a powerful technology that you can use to improve both your own life and the lives of all those that you come in contact with. It can be used in business, education, therapy and for personal growth. I am fortunate to have been practicing NLP for over 30 years. I developed Time Codes and have conducted 36 NLP Trainers Trainings. I also have specialised in modelling which is a powerful method for capturing and transferring expertise. This has allowed me to interact with truly remarkable people from Olympic athletes and coaches to world class salesmen and trainers.

Neal Anderson is a world class NLP trainer. You are fortunate to have this book to guide and assist you on your path. It is clear, comprehensive and well referenced. It covers the INLPTA NLP Coach Practitioner syllabus in detail and also includes other useful information on coaching and performance enhancement.

The International NLP Trainers Association is a worldwide network of NLP Trainers who are dedicated to training the highest quality and most professional NLP. To be assured of quality, ethics and professionalism I can only recommend trainings that follow the INLPTA guidelines and that are taught by fully certified INLPTA Trainers like Neal Anderson.

Learning, change and the development of life skills require integration at both conscious and unconscious levels. Effective coaching works simultaneously at both of these levels. Skill development occurs through systematic practice. My advice to you is to practice the powerful NLP coaching skills that you learn at every opportunity that you get. Form a study group and practice the NLP skills every week. If you do this you will not only truly master NLP but you will begin to embody it in your life.

I wish you good luck in your NLP studies and your coaching career

Wyatt L. Woodsmall, Ph.D.

INLPTA Master Trainer,
Master Coach and Master
Modeller and International
Coordinator for INLPTA

Author of 'Timeline Therapy and The Basis of Personality' and
'People Pattern Power - The Nine Keys to Business Success'.

This book is an excellent, well-researched, handbook for anyone in the coaching field wanting to integrate NLP and the SCORE Model into their coaching approach. Neal has done an outstanding job mining some real nuggets that can *take your coaching to the next level*. As you read this book, *look for those nuggets*. You'll be *pleasantly surprised* what you find.

John Overdurf

Master Trainer of NLP, Coaching and Hypnotherapy
Co-Director of the International Institute of Humanistic
Neuro-Linguistic Psychology and Hypnosis.

Author of 'Training Trances' and
'Dreaming Realities'.

OVERVIEW

What the book is (and isn't)

This is a book about coaching. It is for you if you are already a coach or are looking to adopt a coaching approach in the work you do. Specifically it is a book about using NLP as a Coach, particularly in the field of performance. The bookshelves are full of helpful publications that very effectively cover NLP and Coaching. This book is different and is intended as guide that you can dip into to help integrate NLP and coaching.

- It is a book about Coaching and NLP
- It is not a guide to the whole field of NLP
- It is not a manual describing only one way to coach
- It is a handbook of useful skills, attitudes and patterns for successful coaching

This book brings together a selection of NLP tools and approaches and shows you how they can integrate in a coaching conversation. It expands on the SCORE Model developed by Robert Dilts and Todd Epstein and presents it as a framework to structure a coaching conversation. Following the natural process of change gives you an effective system to help people overcome limitations, produce results, increase focus and reach goals in their personal and professional life.

Who this book is for

Whether you are beginning your coaching practice or an experienced coach who wants to add some magic, this book will offer you new ways to support your coaching practice.

"We can learn something new anytime we believe we can"

Virginia Satir

You don't have to be a coach to coach someone. If you are a manager, leader, parent, teacher or trainer and have ever been in a situation where you want to help someone perform at their best, then this book is for you. It includes:

- The 5 essential stages of the natural process of change
- More than 30 practical ways to coach a client to access inner resources
- How values and beliefs underpin lasting motivation
- How to coach using your clients' metaphors
- The keys to coaching techniques like anchoring, reframing & visualisation
- The fundamentals of delivering a coaching programme

What the book will (and won't) do for you

This book is designed to complement and enrich your practice. Coaching is an active process, not an event and a book by itself won't make you a better coach. In the same way, attending a single training course or simply working with clients won't necessarily make you a better coach. What each of them will do however is to complement and enrich each other as core ingredients for developing your attitude and skills to coach effectively.

Learning and applying the models in this book will introduce you to some key NLP approaches and techniques. I have included full references so you can research further and deepen your knowledge in those areas that particularly interest you. Remember practice is the key to learning, as my Karate Sensei regularly says *"practice makes permanent and only perfect practice will make perfect permanent."* I encourage you to take each element described in the book and apply it with as wide a range of people and contexts as you can. You can then build up a map for yourself of the relative strengths of one approach over another.

The knowledge collected on these pages can help you use NLP techniques to coach others more effectively, more elegantly and more thoroughly. The book covers three essential ingredients.

A Foundation for Coaching

I introduce some core attitudes and skills that underpin a NLP approach to coaching. Key topics from NLP Practitioner and NLP Master Practitioner training are brought to life in these pages. If you like what you read and want to discover more I encourage you to explore some of the books outlined in the reference section and attend an INLPTA certified NLP Training.

The Coaching Framework

The heart of the book is the presentation of the SCORE model as a framework for coaching. This generative approach gives great results with short conversations and full coaching sessions. I outline the five steps of the model in depth and show how the approaches can complement and enrich the stages of the GROW model.

Coaching Resources

The main sections are a collection of approaches coaches could use for building empowering states, shifting perspectives, setting goals, building beliefs, leading change, and operating a coaching business. The resources are presented in a pragmatic style designed for the active coach to use as a memory jogger or reference when working with clients. Many pages are written in a suitable form for self-assessment and I encourage you to use these for yourself and with your clients. Please keep the copyright intact.

Why I wrote the book

As I sit here, comfortable at my desk with a little gentle music in the background and dog at my feet, I am looking at the heading for this section and find my mind wondering *"why did I really write this book?"* Certainly some of the possible answers are that it collects all my thoughts of NLP and Coaching together, or because many of the people I have trained have encouraged me to do so (they have also been true to their word and bought a copy of the first edition), or even because I have a lot of experience applying NLP in Coaching and think that my pragmatic approach to writing might be useful to others. In reality, I feel that the answer lies a little closer to home - I believe I am a writer. Perhaps that's not too astounding but as someone who was put in the bottom set for English at school I spent many years thinking that other people's belief in my ability was more important than my own. Writing is a skill that has taken a while to cultivate. Rather like the seeds in a summer meadow, some need a little more space than others to flourish and grow.

Learning about NLP and Coaching has helped me filter what other people say so that I focus on hearing those things that help me help others to achieve their goals. Experiencing NLP Coaching has supported my natural development and growth. I evolved my style through management and leadership roles in organisations, small charities and in local government. Training has helped too, not least to become a INLPTA Registered NLP, Coaching and Business Communications Trainer, Qualified Teacher and Registered UKCP Psychotherapist, as well as courses with inspirational teachers like Richard Bandler, John Grinder and Robert Holden. Over the past 20 years I have worked with young people and adults and I can say that:

- I coach to make a positive difference with people.
- I wrote this book to help people who coach to make a positive difference with people.

Please dip into the following pages and use whatever resonates with you and your clients, discard that which does not fit and, whatever results you get, do let me know how you get on with your coaching. May I suggest that it is because you are human you have the inner potential to be amazing - have a great life bringing the best out of yourself and others.

Terminology

Throughout the book I have chosen to refer to the person that you are coaching as the client. Of course this could equally well of been the word coachee, or anything else for that matter. It is a construct purely for the purpose of writing. In reality using the name of the person is always the best way to refer to whomever you are coaching!

1

Why Coach?

"There is no medicine like hope, no incentive so great, and no tonic so powerful as expectation of something better tomorrow."

Orison Swett Marden

THE BENEFITS OF COACHING

Coaching is an approach that recognises that each person has within themselves all the resources they need to grow and develop. Coaching can help unlock potential and help others to develop a greater sense of self-efficacy and self-esteem. Working with a coach allows people to explore an area of interest in as much or as little detail as they need in order to identify and put into action the emotional states, thinking patterns, beliefs and behaviours that will help them achieve their goals in work and life.

The Role of the Coach

The coaches role is to direct the conversation towards the client's goals in the spirit of mutual respect and in an honest, safe environment between the coach and client. As a coach you facilitate change through questions, reflections, explanations, stories, metaphors, tasks, guiding attention, exercises, etc.

The principal aim of coaching is to help the people you work with to reach their outcomes - to produce results, increase focus and reach goals in their professional and personal lives.

> *"Coaching is the art of conversationally creating a context for change to occur naturally"*
>
> John Overdurf &
> Julie Silverthorn

> *"Coaching is an opportunity to have a conversation we otherwise wouldn't be having"*
>
> Robert Holden

Inspiring Change

Change is one of the constants in business and life. From the shifting political and economic landscape to the regeneration of our body and the turning of the seasons, change is all around us. One question to consider is *"are we adapting to change or trying to make change adapt to us?"* Coaching can help people recognise and respond positively to change and discover the potential inside themselves to react in an empowering and resourceful way.

Making a Difference

The focus of coaching can be thought about in one of two ways - remedial coaching and generative coaching. **Remedial coaching** has a focus on overcoming challenges, fixing problems and finding solutions. **Generative coaching** has a focus on awareness, improvement, empowerment and building resources for the future. Each coaching programme you may be involved in may focus in just one area or have a little of both.

- What coaching needs do you meet as a coach?
- What balance of remedial to generative coaching do you provide?

Applying Coaching

There are many different ways to look at applying coaching. For me the first fundamental distinction is between using coaching as a tool or approach and seeing coaching as a product or service. To be effective as a coach it helps to be clear about how you define the coaching you provide.

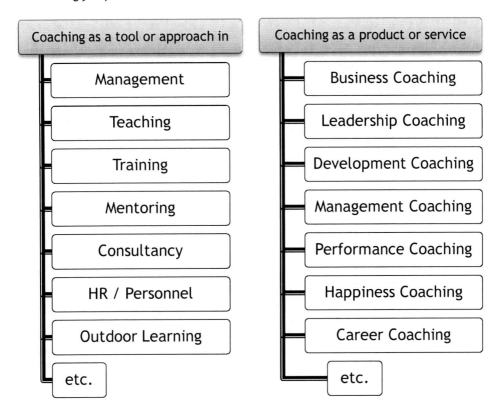

Coaching as a tool or approach in
- Management
- Teaching
- Training
- Mentoring
- Consultancy
- HR / Personnel
- Outdoor Learning
- etc.

Coaching as a product or service
- Business Coaching
- Leadership Coaching
- Development Coaching
- Management Coaching
- Performance Coaching
- Happiness Coaching
- Career Coaching
- etc.

Content vs. Process

For me, coaching is most powerful when it is a fundamentally non-directive or facilitative approach. With this style the coach can easily attend to the structure and sequence of the coaching - tracking the experience of the client and asking questions, opening possibilities and guiding the process of learning and change. The client remains in control of the content - identifying the outcomes, options, resources and actions that will help them achieve their goals.

COACHING DEFINITIONS

Listening to others describe NLP Coaching is always a very popular and beneficial part of my 4 day Coach Training programmes. The definitions vary and all illustrate each coach's approach to one degree or another. Here is my definition:

> *"Helping people reveal their inner potential and put into action the emotional states, thinking patterns, beliefs and behaviours that will help them achieve their goals"*

Some further definitions include:

> Coaching is a non psycho-therapeutical ongoing interaction between a coach and a client that helps the client to **produce results and reach goals in his or her personal and professional life.** The coach facilitates change through verbal and non-verbal communication (i.e., questions, reflections, explanations, stories, metaphors, tasks, guiding attention, exercises, etc.) Through the process of coaching, the client deepens his or her learning, improves his or her performance, and enhances his or her quality of life.
>
> *(International Neuro Linguistic Programming Trainers Association)*

> A **collaborative solution-focused, results-orientated and systematic process** in which the coach facilitates the enhancement of work performance, life experience, self-directed learning and personal growth of the coachee. (Anthony Grant, University of Sydney, 2000)
>
> *(Association for Coaching)*

> Coaching concentrates on where clients are now and what they are willing to do to get where they want to be in the future. **Results are a matter of the client's intentions, choices and actions,** supported by the coach's efforts and application of the coaching process.
>
> *(International Coach Federation)*

> Developing a person's skills and knowledge so that their job performance improves, hopefully leading to the achievement of organisational objectives. It **targets high performance and improvement** at work, although it may also have an impact on an individual's private life. It usually lasts for a short period and focuses on specific skills and goals
>
> *(Chartered Institute of Personnel and Development)*

Some of the other ways of working with people which can complement a coaching approach include:

Mentoring

A relationship in which a more experienced colleague uses their greater knowledge and understanding of the work or workplace to **support the development** of a more junior or inexperienced member of staff.

(Chartered Institute of Personnel and Development)

Training

Organised activity aimed at imparting information and/or instructions to improve the recipient's performance or to help him or her attain a required level of knowledge or skill.

(BusinessDictionory.com)

Consulting

The provision of expert professional advice.

(Hutchinson Encyclopaedic Dictionary)

Counselling

By listening attentively and patiently the counsellor can begin to perceive the difficulties from the client's point of view and can **help them to see things more clearly**, possibly from a different perspective. Counselling is a way of enabling choice or change or of reducing confusion. It does not involve giving advice or directing a client to take a particular course of action.

(British Association for Counselling and Psychotherapy)

Psychotherapy

Psychotherapy aims to help **clients gain insight** into their difficulties or distress, establish a greater understanding of their motivation, and enable them to find more appropriate ways of coping or bring about **changes in their thinking and behaviour.** Psychotherapy involves exploring feelings, beliefs, thoughts and relevant events, sometimes from childhood and personal history, in a structured way with someone trained to help you do it safely.

Psychotherapy is not a magical cure, it is a process to help you **find the capacity for improvement within yourself.**

(UK Council for Psychotherapy)

THE DIMENSIONS OF COACHING

Coaching is something that everyone can do, and often naturally does. NLP Coaching is one of many different approaches you can use to help individuals, groups and teams perform at their best. Before you begin, it is wise to ensure coaching is the most appropriate approach for the current situation.

One way of looking at the range of options to help someone is to consider two different areas of focus.

- The **outcome continuum** could vary between improving performance and confidence in their abilities to achieve tasks and goals **or** improving self and elements of their self-concept, identity and self-esteem.
- The **style continuum** could vary from a focus on content where the style might be more directive to help people gain the knowledge and skills required **or** it could be more process focussed where the style is facilitative, guiding the client to discover their own insights, solutions and actions.

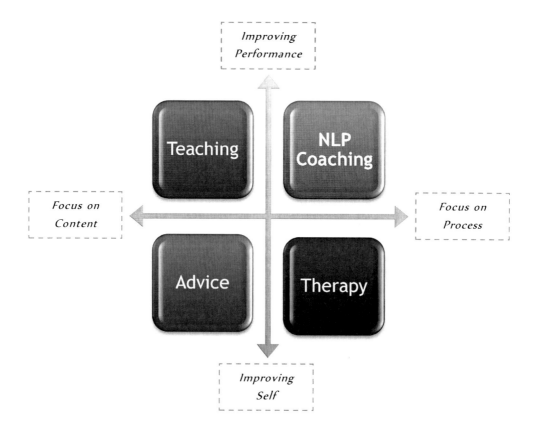

These two continuums give four different approaches for how you could assist a person to resolve a current problem or improve performance in a particular situation.

For example:

"A manager is frustrated that a member of staff is consistently late to meetings"

Advice Approach	*Tell the manager to make an example of the employee or start disciplinary procedures.*
Teaching Approach	*Run training sessions on running effective meetings, time management and possibly stress or anger management.*
Therapeutic Approach	*Resolve the root cause of the manager's frustration and assist them to reveal their inner potential as a manager and support others to do the same.*
Coaching Approach	*Ask the manager what they want in this situation and help them identify the resources needed to get their chosen outcome and achieve the results they want.*

These four approaches are illustrations of the many choices available. The right approach is the one that best fits the needs of the individuals involved (manager, employee and coach), the organisation and the constraints of the situation (time, money, others involved etc.)

Sometimes it can be apparent as the coaching progresses that that client does not have a piece of specific knowledge or skills to achieve their chosen outcome. In this situation the ability of the coach to step out of their coaching role and into the role of teacher, trainer or mentor to deliver the identified knowledge or skills can be

> *Give a man a fish and you feed him for a day.*
> *Teach a man to fish and you feed him for a lifetime.*
>
> *Chinese Proverb*

very beneficial to their clients overall development. Knowing when it is most appropriate to give a person a fish and when best to teach them to fish is an essential part of being a skilled people helper.

Useful questions to consider when selecting your approach include:

- Can I adopt a coaching approach when it best fits the situation?
- Can I step out of my coaching role and into another approach when appropriate?
- Can I choose which approach is most likely to lead to the most generative and long lasting benefits for my client?

THE ESSENTIAL QUALITIES OF A COACH

To be a successful coach requires a combination of knowledge, skills and attitude. Being world class in your chosen field may not make you a great coach, but a great coach can help someone be world class performer.

Rate yourself against these qualities: ✓

○ A genuine interest and passion for helping others

○ An interest in personal development - for yourself and others

○ The ability to be patient, non-judgmental and accept people as they are

○ The flexibility to motivate, inspire and set an example for your clients

○ The creativity to assist people to access their own inner resources

○ A focus on helping people achieve goals and high performance

○ The ability to keep confidentiality and operate ethically

Reflexivity

Being a reflexive coach is a combination of two important skills. First is the ability to replay and reflect on experiences where you have adopted a coaching approach. Secondly, the ability to be critical about your thoughts, actions and feelings will allow you to evaluate what works and identify areas for development.

In general, I have found that focussing about 80% on positives (doing more of what works) and 20% on development areas (doing something different) is a good motivational balance for most people. Focussing too much on areas to develop can lead to self criticism and feelings of overwhelm, inadequacy and confusion where to start. Similarly, focussing entirely on positives from the past can lead to complacency and stagnation. Use your positive strengths even more to provide the energy to make the changes you want to make.

- Which of the above qualities are you best at?
- How did you develop your abilities in that area?
- How can you use that quality even more?
- Which quality do you want to develop further?
- What support do you need to do that?
- What is your next step to take?

CORE CONDITIONS FOR COACHING

For coaching to be successful three core conditions must be met; the client or group must want to change, have the chance to change and know how to change.

Want to

> The client or group must want to make the change. Coaching relies on the person being committed to make a change so that they experience less problems and/or more success. If the person is not motivated in some way then coaching may not be the best approach.
> - Do you want to improve your performance?
> - Are you motivated to change the way things have been?
> - How ready are you to do what you need to do to solve this problem?

Chance to

> We all live and work as a part of a larger system. Successful coaching occurs when a person has the right knowledge, space and time to develop and improve. If the person does not have the chance to change themselves or the system, then coaching may not be the best approach.
> - What opportunity do you have to put the changes you will make into practice?
> - If you make a change, will your team / family / community support you?

How to

> Coaching helps people recognise how they can use their inner resources and external support to help them make the change they want. If the person does not know how to make the change they want, or use the resources they have available to them, then mentoring, teaching or training may be a useful addition to coaching.
> - Are you willing to do what you need to do to improve?
> - Are you willing to learn how to make the improvements you want?

PERFORMANCE COACHING

Whether you are involved in management, leadership, coaching, mentoring, sports or any task or behaviour, performance has three elements. Firstly you need to develop the technical skills and capabilities to perform consistently at your chosen level. Secondly you need the mental strength and strategies to be able to use all your skills. And thirdly, you need to have the physical health and endurance to be able to use those skills when you need to.

World class performance occurs when there is a full release of inner potential. Skills and abilities that have been learnt through conscious diligent practice can be applied with creativity, fluidity and grace. With a clear goal and a focussed attitude, we all have the potential to be world class in whatever field we choose.

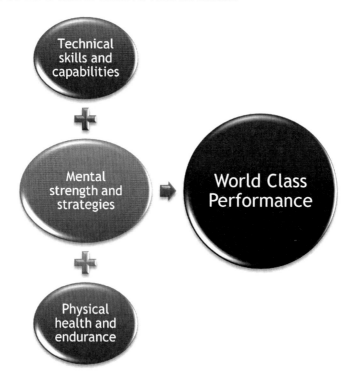

Coaching world class performance is about helping clients build the mental strength to make the most of, and further develop, their technical skills and physical heath. This book describes some key NLP approaches, including the SCORE model, which can be applied to help people develop world class mental strength.

- In what field will you coach people to perform to their potential?
- In what field would you like to perform to your potential?

High performers are usually already doing many things well, that is of course why they are high performers. For those people who are not yet performing at a level they want to, coaching can help them celebrate and further develop their strengths and release their potential.

Performance = Potential – Interference

In the 1970's Tim Gallwey introduced the concept of the Inner Game, the area of focus where a person's performance is the result of their inner potential less any interference. Gallwey suggested that more often than not, in any area from sports to business, it is the mental processes going on in our Inner Game that provide the interference that limits performance. In short, thinking gets in the way of performing.

> *"Coaching is unlocking a person's potential to maximise their own performance. It is helping them to learn rather than teaching them."*
>
> Timothy Gallwey

Performance coaching assists your client to reduce any unhelpful thinking and self doubt that may get in the way of performing to their potential.

- The coach supports the client to take response-ability for where they are
- The coach assists the client to be clear about where they want to be
- The coach and client work together on reducing interference to performance
- The coach and client work together on building performance strengths

Excellence Comes From Awareness

Performance excellence is only ever a moment in time. If we recognise the present situation and are non-judgmental we can be fully aware of what we are seeing, hearing, feeling, smelling and tasting in the moment. By following the advice of Fritz Perls to *"lose your mind and come to your senses"* we can let go of the need for more training, experience and the pressure to 'try harder'.

Freeing ourselves from unhelpful past habits and future demands means that achieving world class performance becomes instinctive. The potential within us is able to be realised with an unconscious natural ease. When we trust ourselves and our abilities to embrace the challenges we face, we can achieve the peak performance state of flow.

- Are you aware of the potential and wisdom inside you?
- Can you trust the potential and wisdom inside you?
- Are you willing to perform to your potential?

Celebrating Strengths

Strengths are areas of performance that are well developed. They are often the result of deliberate practice, but that does not mean they are areas where a person is performing to their potential.

> *If you only plan to work on your weaknesses, you are only planning to be average*
>
> *Neal Anderson*

The field of positive psychology has shown that by focussing on what a person is doing well, that area becomes even better and, more often than not, many areas where they are less strong seem to naturally resolve themselves. A 2002 study by the Corporate Leadership Council of 19,187 employees from 34 organisations found that when managers emphasised performance strengths, performance was 36.4% higher, and when they emphasised personality strengths, performance was 21.3% higher. In contrast, emphasising weaknesses led to a 26.8% decline for performance weaknesses and a 5.5% decline for personality weaknesses.

- Where are you placing your attention when you coach others?
- What strengths do you have as a coach?
- What strengths do your clients have?

Choosing Success

Many people are aware of how events in the past have shaped their experiences and motivations in the present. Equally important, is the understanding that what is happening in the present can directly influence what happens in our future.

Coaching supports people to set outcomes and build the emotional states, thinking patterns and empowering beliefs in the present that enable them to carry out the behaviours required to achieve their goals in the present and the future.

- Are you helping clients appreciate where they are right now?
- Are you helping your clients take responsibility for where they want to go?
- Are you helping your clients take action and move forward?

2

A Foundation for NLP Coaching

"Think twice before you speak, because your words and influence will plant the seed of either success or failure in the mind of another"

Napoleon Hill

WE CONSTRUCT OUR REALITY

Each of us is unique in the way we relate to ourselves and the world. Our individual thoughts, feelings and actions are shaped by our neurological make-up, our social background and our personal history.

The Map Is Not the Territory

The experiences we have lead us to construct our own model or map of the way things are in the world – what opportunities there are, what skills we have and what is truly important. We use our map of the world to guide us and make decisions about what information to pay attention to, what we should and shouldn't do and what an experience means.

- Our experience of the world is directed by the map of reality we hold in our mind, not reality itself

Our maps bring forth opportunity and possibility and it can be the very same ones that prove prisons for some people. If we update our map and change our filters on experience we can update what it is possible for us to achieve.

> *"Human beings live in the real world. We do not, however, operate directly or immediately on that world, but rather we operate with a map or series of maps that we use to guide our behaviour. These maps or representation systems necessarily differ from the territory that they model... When people come to us in therapy expressing pain and dissatisfaction, the limitations they experience are typically in their representation of the world not in the world itself"*
>
> **Bandler and Grinder**
> (The Structure of Magic)

> *"As modelers, we're not interested in whether what we offer you is true or not, whether it's accurate or whether it can be neurologically proven to be accurate, an actual representation of the world. We're only interested in what works"*
>
> **Bandler and Grinder**
> (Frogs into Princes P18)

Discovering your Clients Map of the World

Modelling is the process of discovering how a person gets the results they get. It includes how they think, the representational systems, language patterns and the physiology they adopt. It also contains explicit information of the steps to be taken in what order to obtain a given outcome.

NLP has grown by modelling excellent performers in a field. The same tools can be used to model how people remain stuck in problems or create lives that are unfulfilled. Knowing how a person gets the results they do, you can often intervene effectively by educating them how to stop themselves doing what they don't want and start generating more desirable and compelling behaviours.

EXPERIENCE IS SUBJECTIVE

There are three areas of subjective experience - thinking processes, emotional states and behaviour. These three processes are connected and interact with and influence each other. If you change an internal emotional state, it shows up in external behaviour: people move differently, have changes in muscle tone, respiration, flesh tint and tempo. If you change an internal thinking process, the eyes move and other gestures change. If you change beliefs, you feel, think and act differently.

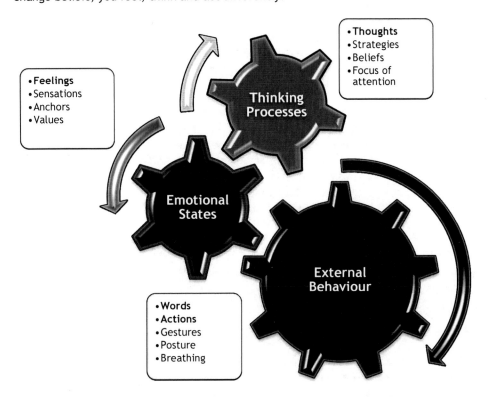

- **Thoughts**
- **Strategies**
- **Beliefs**
- **Focus of attention**

Thinking Processes

- **Feelings**
- Sensations
- Anchors
- Values

Emotional States

External Behaviour

- **Words**
- **Actions**
- Gestures
- Posture
- Breathing

What is the simplest change that will have the most impact for your client?
Coaching involves helping a person recognise how their current actions, internal thinking processes and emotional state have influenced their current situation. Through coaching your client identifies ways to make changes so that they can carry out the behaviours necessary to achieve their goals.

- Thinking processes drive emotional states.
- Emotional states drive behaviour.
- If what you are doing is working, do more of it.
- If what you are doing isn't working, change it to something better.

YOUR REALITY IS YOUR CHOICE

We construct our own reality from our unique neurology, social background, and personal history. We can use our free will to construct our present and future experiences, as William James has said *"My first act of free will shall be to believe in free will. I will go a step further with my will, not only act with it, but believe as well; believe in my individual reality and creative power."*

- Believing you can choose your thoughts and feelings means you can choose your present and future

There are two principal beliefs we can hold regarding the present and future events of our life. We can believe the event is the result of some **cause,** accept response-ability for the situation and choose our response – I can change, I am in control of myself, I have the freedom to respond in the most appropriate way. If we focus on responding to the consequences of the event we may limit our choices by believing we are 'at-**effect'** – because of what's happened I have no control, they make me feel this way, the world does this to me. Often clients (and coaches) can feel stuck in their particular situation because they are 'at-effect'. Believing we are 'at-cause' means we can be proactive about our life.

- If you could be any way you want, how would you be?
- In order to perform at your best what else do you need?
- What would you like more of in your work, life or relationships?

Being Proactive

The choice to be proactive is described by the psychiatrist Victor Frankl in 'Man's Search for Meaning' as the choice of a person to take responsibility for his or her life, rather than looking for reason in outside circumstances or in other people. During his time in Nazi concentration camps Frankl endured indignities, torture and

> *"Between stimulus and response there is a space. In that space is our power to choose our response. In our response lies our growth and our freedom."*
>
> *Viktor Frankl*

never knew from one moment to the next if he would be sent to the ovens or be one of the 'saved' ones. He lost his wife, mother, father and family. Frankl concluded that even under the worst circumstances people can make and find their own meaning;

"Everything can be taken from a man but ...the last of the human freedoms - to choose one's attitude in any given set of circumstances, to choose one's own way."

Being proactive is about accepting that you are the only one who is guaranteed to have the ability to change your life. Proactivity is more than merely taking the initiative or just putting a positive spin on things. It means that as a human being we are responsible for our lives, our behaviour is a function of our decisions not our conditions. We have the initiative and the response-ability to make things happen.

You hurt me	Dis-empowers – there is nothing you can do about it now
I felt hurt by you	Empowers – you can choose to have a different emotion if you want

Proactive At Cause

- "Let's look at what we can do"
- "I can do this"
- "I choose"
- "I am in control of my feelings"
- "I can do things differently"
- "I can choose the responses I make"
- "I am going to learn what I need"

- "There's nothing I can do"
- "That's the way I am"
- "I have to do this"
- "They do that to me"
- "It's not my fault"
- "It's just an automatic response"
- "It's just my learning style"

Reactive At Effect

"The therapist's task is to challenge the [client's] model in some way which assists clients in taking responsibility for their responses"

Bandler & Grinder

Whenever you point a finger there are always three fingers pointing back at you. Being 'at cause' and using proactive language puts our actions within our influence. It does not put the problem 'out there'. It identifies the part of the problem that is 'in here'.

- How have you chosen to respond to the situation?
- What can you choose to change within yourself to improve the situation?

PERCEPTION IS A PROJECTION

We create our own reality - what we see, hear, touch, taste and smell in the outside world is translated via our neurology into an internal representation which directs our ongoing internal states, thinking processes and external behaviours. As this translation occurs our memories, values, beliefs, hopes and fears directly influence our internal representations and our external perceptions.

> *"Projection is an unconscious, automatic process whereby a content that is unconscious to the subject transfers itself to an object"*
>
> Carl Jung
> *(Archetypes and the Collective Unconscious)*

- Whatever we notice in the external world is a reflection of our internal unconscious processes

We recognise outside us what resonates inside of us

Our perception is a projection of our unconscious processes, particularly those processes used to understand and make meaning from peoples actions, behaviours and communications. Since we can never truly know another human beings experience (we haven't lived their life with their body) the best we can do is to apply our own map of the world to assist in the process of understanding. As we do this we '*project*' ourselves onto the world and end up seeing things not as <u>they</u> are, but as <u>we</u> are. All the positive qualities we see in others are a projection of our positive qualities and strengths. Similarly all the less helpful qualities we notice in others are also a projection of our inner qualities or conflicts.

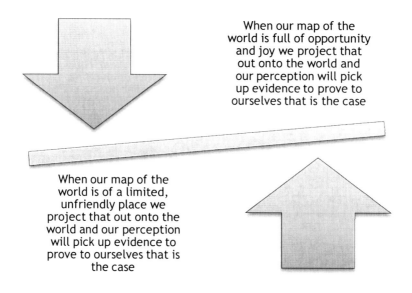

When our map of the world is full of opportunity and joy we project that out onto the world and our perception will pick up evidence to prove to ourselves that is the case

When our map of the world is of a limited, unfriendly place we project that out onto the world and our perception will pick up evidence to prove to ourselves that is the case

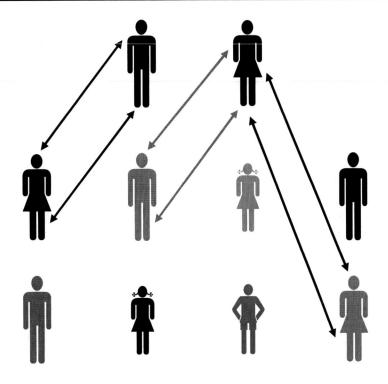

Be careful what you look for because you will find it

Holding the idea that 'perception is a projection' as true means that we are completely empowered to change anything (and everything) in our world. Whenever a person is noticing an unhelpful pattern or quality in others, all they need do is look inside and discover what they may need to think or believe differently such that their perception of the outside world changes.

- How aware are you of your own map of the world?
- What aspects of your own personality are you noticing in others?
- What qualities do you admire in others? Do you recognise them in yourself?
- What qualities do you dislike in others? Do you recognise them in yourself?
- When you are coaching what beliefs or expectations are you projecting?
- When you are coaching what beliefs or expectations do you notice your clients projecting?

CONSCIOUS & UNCONSCIOUS MINDS

In NLP the metaphor of the conscious mind is used to represent those things we are aware of in any one moment (about 7± 2 chunks of information) and the unconscious mind to represent everything else. All our experiences, memories, skills, beliefs and values are held in our unconscious mind and we bring them to consciousness when it is appropriate. Our conscious and unconscious minds are like two sides of the same coin.

- Most high performance states have very little conscious processing
- Structured, diligent practice at a conscious level enables unconscious learning
- Coaching with the unconscious mind in agreement will lead to lasting change
- Congruence is a conscious and unconscious commitment to an action or goal

Conscious and Unconscious Integration

A person may come to coaching to consciously make a change or improve performance, however if the pattern of behaviour they are engaging in is happening automatically, it will be an unconscious process. There will be conscious and unconscious elements of the pattern. For coaching to be successful in the long term the coach and client must work with both elements. Milton Erickson would say that the reason his clients had problems was because their conscious and unconscious minds were out of rapport.

> "therapy should be orientated equally about the conscious and unconscious, since integration of the total personality is the desired goal"
>
> Milton Erickson

- Successful change happens at an unconscious level with direction and support from our conscious mind

Conscious thinking processes	vs.	Unconscious thinking processes
Setting outcomes and taking steps towards what matters		Feeling drawn to be your true self and do what is truly important
Reasoning something through		Sleeping on a problem and solving it overnight
Trying to remember a name or location and not being able to do it		Stopping thinking about something and the answer just pops us
Working with someone who is stuck and helping them think or decide what to do next		Working with someone and creating the space for a moment of insight and understanding
Giving someone some well thought out advice only to get the response "that wouldn't work"		Telling a story about something seemingly unrelated when a person suddenly solves their own problem

Your conscious mind excels at

- Making plans and setting outcomes
- Analysis and critical thinking
- Holding a narrow focus
- Processing sequentially using language
- Giving your unconscious mind a direction to follow, rather like the captain of a ship sets the course.

Your unconscious mind is excellent at

- Making links and associations
- Operating with learned patterns and habits
- Storing memories, decisions, beliefs, values
- Running your body according to a higher wisdom
- Working creatively and holistically using metaphor
- Accepting direction from the conscious mind by listening to all you think and say and bringing it to pass according to belief, rather like the crew efficiently running the ship.

Unlimited Potential

We learn in many ways, including cognition and thought, direct experience and by creating possible scenarios in our mind. Through the processes of acquisition, consolidation and retrieval it can be helpful to believe that every memory, belief, decision and skill resides in our unconscious mind as part of our map of the world. Coaching the conscious mind can create a clear direction for the unconscious to follow.

- Every learned resource is stored as a particular network of neural connections.

Dr Paul Goodwin has estimated we have the potential for 10 to the power of 10 to the power of 11 different neural connections in our mind and body; more than all the stars in the sky or the number of grains of sand on the entire planet. We will only use one 10th of all these possible connections in our life. In a practical sense, we have unlimited potential for how we construct and can re-construct our model the world.

$$10^{10^{11}}$$

- Bringing what is unconscious to consciousness enables people to re-evaluate past associations and make choices that lead to achieving their outcomes
- Placing what is conscious into the unconscious enables people to habitually perform in a state of excellence

HELPFUL BELIEFS FOR COACHES

Throughout their early seminars several helpful assumptions are presented by Richard Bandler and John Grinder. They are a guiding set of beliefs that help define the NLP attitude and approach. In practice, adopt the belief and notice what results you get. If you like the results continue to hold the belief; if you don't, change it to something more useful.

- Which beliefs are helpful for you to hold?
- Which beliefs are helpful for coaching change?
- Which beliefs are helpful for coaching performance?
- What additional beliefs do you hold that support your coaching?

> "Everything we are going to tell you here is a lie. Since we have no claim to truth or accuracy we will be lying to you consistently. There are only two differences between us and other teachers: One is that we announce at the beginning of our seminars that everything we say will be a lie, and other teachers do not. The other difference is that most of our lies will work out really well if you act as if they were true"
>
> *Bandler and Grinder*
> (Frogs into Princes)

There are several different groupings of these NLP Presuppositions in the NLP literature. There is no definitive list. The following selection can be particularly applicable to Coaching.

We process information through our senses

Our experience at any moment can be represented through the visual, auditory, kinaesthetic, olfactory, and gustatory senses.

Having a choice is better than not having a choice

The person with the most flexibility is able to exert the most control in system. (The law of requisite variety, taken from Ashby in cybernetics, control and systems theory). Act to build flexibility and increase choice in your model of the world. The more choices you have, the freer you are and the more influence you can have.

Mind and body are two parts of the same system

Each affects the other - it is not possible to make a change in one without the other being affected. Our mind and body are different expressions of one person; they interact and mutually influence each other.

The meaning of your communication is in the response you get

If you are not getting the results you intended be flexible and be prepared to do something different. Whenever the response is different to the one you wanted take responsibility for making communication effective.

People make the best choice they can at the time

Our decisions are based on what is important to us and the information available in our model of the world. We always make the best choice we can. Sometimes the choice may be self-defeating, bizarre or harmful, but in that moment it seems the best way forward.

Every behaviour has a positive intention

In every action we seek to achieve something of benefit to us, whether we are conscious of it or not. Our behaviour is not random, even though sometimes it may seem like it. The intention or purpose behind an action is separate to the action itself. When a person has a better choice of behaviour that also achieves their positive intention, they can take it.

There is no failure, only feedback.

Notice the results you are getting and either do more of what works or change what you are doing. Our specific thoughts, actions, and feelings consistently produce specific results. We may be happy or unhappy with these results, but if we repeat the same thoughts, actions, and feelings, we'll get the same results. The process works perfectly, whatever we do or don't do **results are guaranteed.**

All meanings are context dependent

We make meaning of the world based on our own model of the world; every behaviour has value in some context. What we decide an event means depends on the situation and how we filter the information we receive.

People work perfectly

No one is wrong or broken - our strategies are sometimes useful and sometimes less useful. At a fundamental level we are all OK and have within us the potential and drive to achieve our goals in life. Whenever we are not getting the results we want then it is the strategy we are using that is not working. Help people find and use existing successful strategies in new situations or change an ineffective strategy for something better.

We have all the resources we need, or we can create them

We have unlimited potential within us for creating resourceful states, learning and being our true self. We are more than our problems and we have, within us, the answers and solutions to life's challenges.

CONNECTING WITH YOUR CLIENT

Since people have different maps of the world, as a coach it is important to be able to understand the other person's situation as accurately as possible. One way to do this is to enter the other person's map of reality. Another way is by using sensory grounded information in terms of what can be seen, heard, and felt.

Many people are in the habit of describing what they see, hear or feel in interpretive terms and give meaning to other's behaviour that may or may not be accurate. For example, a person might see a certain look on someone's face and describe that person as unfriendly, mean, angry, or upset. This process of mind reading is a non-sensory based assumption. If they ask that person what is going on, they may discover that the person is actually is in physical pain or is in a different state altogether.

> "By hallucination we are not implying a value judgement... simply that when a therapist decides without checking with the client what the non verbal message is in words, he is assuming that the meaning of that posture or gesture is the same as it is in his own model of the world"
>
> *Bandler & Grinder*
> *(The Structure of Magic II)*

Calibration

Being able to notice the sensory distinctions in someone's communication is essential in order to be able to calibrate whether your work is progressing successfully. Calibration allows you to define your client's expressions by comparing their present behaviour with their previously observed behaviour. It is especially important in detecting congruence (or incongruence) within your client. Use calibration, checking with the client and sensory based descriptions as much as possible when coaching.

> "The highest quality information is behavioural. Our direct experience, or what we call sensory grounded information, is the highest possible quality"
>
> *John Grinder*
> *& Michael McMaster*
> *(Precision)*

Rapport

Rapport has been described as the ability to build a bridge of harmony or trust between people. It can be considered a sympathetic relationship or understanding, the process of making a 2-way connection with someone else or experiencing a genuine sense of trust and respect with another person. As you adjust the features of your communication style to match the person with whom you are relating, an unconscious message is sent to the other person. That person receives the message "this person is like me."

Professor Albert Mehrabian has studied the relative importance of verbal and nonverbal messages with a particular focus on face to face communication of feelings and attitudes – do we like or dislike the person delivering the message. His results suggest that when talking about feelings or attitudes, 7% of 'total liking' is the result of the words that we say, or the content of our communication. 38% of 'total liking' is a result of our verbal behaviour, which includes tone of voice, timbre, tempo, and volume and 55% of 'total liking' is a result of our nonverbal communication, body posture, breathing, skin colour and movement.

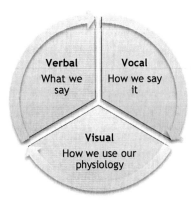

Whilst these percentages do not hold in general communication or when delivering information, what does matter is that coaches are aware of and can be responsive to all the ways that they communicate with clients.

Pacing and Leading

Pacing can be considered the ongoing process of establishing and maintaining rapport. It is a way of acknowledging another person and meeting them in their map of the world. You can use your body to pace breathing, rhythm, gestures, energy and movements (or lack of them); pace the voice tone, tempo, volume, key words, representational systems and predicates and pace a person's ongoing experience with what you are saying.

Pace Content	Pace Communication Patterns
• Take a genuine interest in the other person • Talk about something "in common" • Be willing to see the world from their point of view • Use the other persons key words and phrases	• Breath at the same rate as the other person • Match voice speed, tone and volume • Use the same representational system (VAK) words • Very subtly mirror body position, gestures & movement

In coaching pacing is often essential to establish rapport to begin with, but you will pretty soon want to lead the other person to a new state otherwise there might be two people exquisitely stuck, confused or angry etc. When you have a clear outcome agreed you can lead your client in discovering how they can achieve their chosen outcome.

- Lead with physiology and voice by changing posture, energy levels, movement, voice tone or volume
- Lead with language by using a coaching question or statement

LISTENING AND OBSERVING

The skill of listening is a powerful tool that can help people feel valued and whole. Not being listened to, especially when you have something important you want to say can lead to unhelpful emotions like anger and frustration. Being able to listen to what people are truly saying is a core skill for coaches.

True listening provides the most appropriate conditions for your client to hear themselves think, as Hermann Hesse has said *"everything becomes a little different as soon as it is spoken out loud."* Often the act of being listened to with empathy, congruence and unconditional positive regard will allow people to access the inner resources they need to grow, develop and meet the challenges they are facing.

Listening to Understand

In their book 'Heart Work' Claus Møller and Reuvon Bar-On describe five different levels of listening we all use. Each has its value in different contexts however Level 5 - Empathetic listening is most appropriate for coaching.

Empathetic listening involves seeing the world from your clients point of view and listening with curiosity to understand. Listening in this way does not involve judgement. It usually has a minimum of internal dialogue and involves:

- Listening with
  Your ears
  Your eyes
  Your heart

- Listening to
  The words
  The tone of voice
  The body language

- Listening for
  Emotions
  Behaviour
  Meanings

Empathetic Listening   **5**
Listening to the words, the emotions and the body language to understand

Attentive Listening   **4**
Paying undivided attention and focussing on the words

Selective Listening   **3**
Hearing certain parts of the conversation that interest us

Pretending Listening   **2**
Asking questions but not really being interested in the answers

Ignoring   **1**
Not really listening—our body is there but our mind is somewhere else

Silence Works

By practicing empathetic listening you are providing a context for the client to get their thoughts out of their head and into the room where they can be examined, changed or even let go. The normal flow of everyday conversation goes something like: you say a bit, pause – I say a bit, pause – you say a bit more, pause – I say a bit more etc. The balance of talking to listening is about 50/50. In a coaching conversation the balance is much more towards 80/20 with the client talking, answering questions and explaining their situation, thoughts, feelings and ideas.

More often than not, if the coach holds a supportive space and is comfortable with silence then the client will fill that space with valuable words which otherwise would not have been said.

Semantically Packed Words

In "Science and Sanity" (1933) Alfred Korzybski defines a semantic response as the **total** response, neurological, emotional, cognitive, semantic and behavioural, to a thing or event. When a person with a spider phobia is frightened by a spider, their semantic response is their nervous behaviour, the electricity in their nerves, the chemicals in their blood - everything they do in reacting to the spider!

> "That's a great deal to make one word mean" Alice said in a thoughtful tone. "When I make a word do a lot of work like that," said Humpty Dumpty, "I always pay it extra."
>
> Lewis Carroll
> *(Alice through the Looking Glass)*

A semantically packed (or dense) word is one that triggers a semantic response. When your client hears "that word" spoken in "that way", they automatically recall a version of what they previously heard/saw/felt along with the associated feelings and past meanings.

Paying careful attention to your client will allow you to calibrate to their particular semantic words and phrases. Listen out for a particular phrase, voice tone, volume, emphasis, pause or being spoken through clenched teeth.

- When the client is describing a problem state you can note the words and phrases they use and then use them back to your client to test if they have made the change they want.
- If your client is describing a positive memory, useful belief or resourceful state, using the same words (with the same vocal qualities and associated gestures) will assist your client in further connecting to the resources.

CONGRUENCE

Can you remember a time when you have been having a conversation with someone and they said they were going to do something and you could tell that they weren't really going to do it? Perhaps they said "yes" and also shook their head. Think of another time when you were having a similar conversation and yet you were completely sure the person was going to do what they said, they were committed to taking that action.

- Congruence is when your internal state, your internal processes and your external behaviour are all aligned.
- Congruency occurs when you make a full conscious and unconscious commitment to some outcome or behaviour.

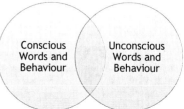

Noticing and Observing Congruence

When people communicate they do so in many different ways. The whole message is made up of many distinct elements, some of which we consciously notice and some that remain out of our conscious awareness. When all the elements fit together and convey the same message communication is congruent. Examples of congruent communication:

- Body relaxed, breathing slow, hands together in lap, soft voice, regular speed of talking, words "I do the things I can to help her; I love her so very much"
- Shoulders tight, one hand by side, one finger pointing, loud and fast speech, words "everything you do turns out to be a complete disaster"

When agreeing the coaching topic, the ethics and ecology check is an essential step in confirming congruence for both you and the client. In fact, **if you are not congruent with the topic, consider doing something different** so you are. Sometimes this may mean changing your approach or defining clear boundaries, sometimes it may mean referring your client or just walking away.

Congruence is particularly important to notice when your client is choosing the coaching topic, confirming they want to make a change, deciding on an outcome, selecting the next smallest step, describing their commitment to take action, etc.

If your client is not congruent with their chosen outcome, whether they say it or you use your sensory acuity to notice it, you should back-up in the process and explore the ecology of the change further before continuing. It is unlikely your client will be able to successfully change unless they are congruent at a conscious and unconscious level.

Recognising Incongruence

When there is a mismatch between some of the elements in the message, the communication is incongruent. There are two types of incongruity:

Simultaneous Incongruity

Where a person is experiencing internal conflict or a shortage of information in their map of the world and two messages are communicated at the same time (mixed messages).

> *"When a boy says to a girl "I love you" he is using words to convey that which is more convincingly conveyed by his tone of voice and his movements, and the girl, if she has any sense, will pay more attention to those accompanying signs than the words"*
>
> *Gregory Bateson*
> *(Steps to an Ecology of Mind)*

 For example a trainer may ask a delegate "*do you understand?*" and receive an answer "*yes*" along with a particular tone of voice and side to side shake of the head that suggests a "*no*".

Sequential Incongruity

In a sequential incongruity the person appears to be congruent in favour of an action at one time and equally congruently against the same action at another time.

enjoyment - regret - enjoyment - regret

For example a person may be keen to give up a long term habit (to lose weight and exercise more) during a coaching session and yet have no desire for change when they are in another context (eating a meal out or working away from home).

Responding to Incongruence

The first stage of dealing with any incongruity is drawing it to the attention of the client "*I noticed when you said _____ you also _____. Those elements don't seem to match to me - what was going on there for you?*" Once you have begun exploring the incongruity you can help your client recognise the emotional states, thinking processes, values or beliefs behind the incongruity and assist them to make the appropriate changes for them.

Incongruent Communication	Response to Incongruent Communication
Body stiff Breathing slow and high in chest Arms crossed Monotone voice Words - "I really do care'"	"I notice that when you spoke your body was stiff, your arms were crossed, you used used a monotone voice and I heard you say you that you really do care. Those elements don't seem to match to me - what was going on there for you?"

Representational Systems

Representational Systems are one of the ways people perceive the world around them. Individuals can have different ways of thinking and communicating their experiences - some express themselves in pictures, others talk about how things sound to them, and others speak about how things feel. The words we use describe how we are representing our reality - they are "how" we are thinking in any moment. It is possible we all have a natural preference for how we describe both our internal and external experience in any situation.

V
- Visual
- Seeing
- Imaging a picture

A
- Auditory
- Hearing
- Imagining sounds

K
- Kinaesthetic
- Touch / feeling
- Imagining feelings

O
- Olfactory
- Smelling
- Imagining smells

G
- Gustatory
- Tasting
- Imagining tastes

Ad
- Internal Dialogue
- Talking to yourself

Matching Representational Systems

By matching a persons representational system language you can gain rapport very quickly at an unconscious level. For example if a person says *"I want to get a **handle** on where the project is at so that the team can work in **harmony** with each other"* the coach may reply by matching the kinaesthetic and auditory representational systems by saying *"would you be interested in discussing how you **feel** about the current situation and **talking** about solutions."* With a group use language that includes all the representational systems in order to appeal to all members of the audience. Examples of words and phrases to use:

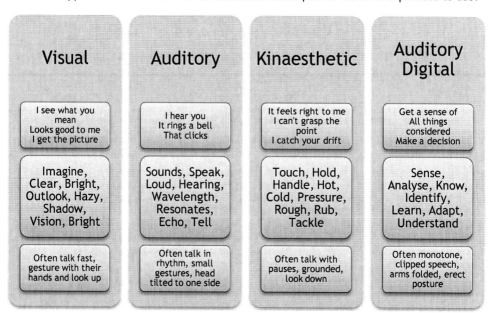

Visual	Auditory	Kinaesthetic	Auditory Digital
I see what you mean Looks good to me I get the picture	I hear you It rings a bell That clicks	It feels right to me I can't grasp the point I catch your drift	Get a sense of All things considered Make a decision
Imagine, Clear, Bright, Outlook, Hazy, Shadow, Vision, Bright	Sounds, Speak, Loud, Hearing, Wavelength, Resonates, Echo, Tell	Touch, Hold, Handle, Hot, Cold, Pressure, Rough, Rub, Tackle	Sense, Analyse, Know, Identify, Learn, Adapt, Understand
Often talk fast, gesture with their hands and look up	Often talk in rhythm, small gestures, head tilted to one side	Often talk with pauses, grounded, look down	Often monotone, clipped speech, arms folded, erect posture

Overlapping Representational Systems

Overlap is the process of pacing and leading a person with language to represent their experience from one representational system to another. It can be a very helpful way of helping a person access a full internal representation and can give a person them a different point of view from which to consider their situation.

> *"We, as therapists, can assist our clients in expanding portions of their representations which impoverish and limit them"*
>
> *Bandler and Grinder*
> (The Structure of Magic II)

- Overlapping can help you create new experiences for your client

For example:

- *"Thinking about the future…*
- *"Make a picture of something you want to achieve in your work or life…"*
- ***"And as you make the image bright and clear, what sounds do you notice…***
- *"What are other people saying and what are you saying to yourself…"*
- ***"And as you listen to yourself, get in touch with your internal sensations…"***
- *"Where does the good feeling start and where does it move to next…"*
- ***"And as you allow those pleasant feelings to grow, start to consider…"***
- *"What is the next smallest step to take to help you achieve your goal?"*

Bringing Memories to Life

Great stories and songs use all the representational systems to enable the listener to create a rich internal representation. Think about a reading book where you were really engrossed, or when you were listening to a great storyteller – did you have a sense of being in the moment, were you there with them?

You can help someone really recall all the details of a particular event by asking them to recall what they saw, what they heard, what they were doing, what they were feeling and what they were saying to themselves.

- When you recall a situation in all the representational systems you relive the experience
- When you imagine a future situation in all the representational systems you make it real

ASKING QUESTIONS

The ability to formulate and ask questions is a key skill in coaching. Questions are used to discover information, clarify details, direct attention, reveal options and transform meaning.

Open Questions

Open questions invite the answerer to consider and respond with information that will describe their model of the world. The most useful questions start with who, what, where, when, and how.

- When exactly is this a problem for you?
- How can you develop your skills and abilities even more?
- What are some of the options you now have?

Closed Questions

Closed questions often invite a single word or yes or no response. They can be used to rule out options, invite decisions and are useful in establishing commitment.

- When will you take the next smallest step?
- Are you committed to doing what you say you want to do?
- Do you have anything else to discuss?

Leading questions

Leading questions should be used with care so as to direct your client to discover options, possibilities and choices, but not offer advice or solutions.

- If you knew the answer to this problem, what would it be?
- When you are feeling at your best, how does that affect your performance?
- If that has answered all of your questions, shall we agree the programme?

Complex Questions

Complex questions are rarely helpful as they give the listener too much to answer in one go. The listener either doesn't know which part of your question is the most important to answer, or they forget all the questions you asked. Ask questions one at a time.

- When are you going to be assertive and find the time to speak directly to the person involved?
- Exactly when and where is the problem from your point of view and are you sure it is actually a problem at all?

Chunking Questions

In order to prevent overwhelm and speed up processing, we tend organise data in to distinct sets or chunks of information. These can be **large chunk** (I'm excited) or **small chunk** (the little toe in my left foot is tingling). Using chunking questions can be useful in gathering complete information and shifting your clients focus of attention to something they hadn't yet fully considered. Using the words your client has said as part of your chunking question will ensure you maintain rapport and don't sound repetitive.

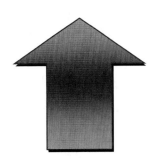

What is this an example of?

Why is that important to you?

Chunking up

Some people are happiest when they have their teeth sunk into all the tiny facts. Sometimes your client can be stuck in the details and it can be helpful to come up for air and see the big picture. Chunking up takes you to a more general category or understanding such as overall purpose or meaning. You can discover a person's motivating values by chunking up.

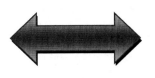

What else?

What are other examples of ____?

Chunking across

Use chunking across to make links and change the context or content of the discussion. Listen out for clients chunking across (that reminds me of...) to avoid something they don't want to talk about.

What is a example of that?

Tell me more, specifically?

Chunking down

Sometimes your client will talk at a very high level covering general ideas and themes. By staying in the general they may be keeping their options open, creating concepts or perhaps be avoiding something. Chunking down allows you to find out more details, fill in the empty gaps and discover the reality of the situation. You can help a person associate into an emotional state by chunking down.

LANGUAGE DESCRIBES EXPERIENCE

We build a model of the world in language that describes (amongst other things) how we take in information, respond to others, make decisions, and learn. The model is used to filter every experience and give each experience meaning. People are generally aware of some elements of their model and are often unconscious of much of it. In coaching, the interference that stops clients achieving their potential performance is typically an unconscious element of their map of the world.

Surface and Deep Structure

The words we use on the surface, what a person actually says, are rarely a complete and accurate representation of their experience. For example, *"I'm scared"* does not reveal what, when or how a person is actually scared. In language the deep structure is the full linguistic representation and usually contains the meaning attached to the experience. For example *"I'm scared of cows"* or *"I'm scared of how good I could really be if I actually achieve this goal."* By revealing the deep structure you can often discover the thinking processes, value or belief that is hidden by the deletion, distortion or generalisation of experience.

- Beneath every surface level statement is a deeper structure meaning

The Meta Model

The Meta Model is a full set of specific questions or language patterns designed to move between surface and deep structure and challenge and expand the limits of a person's model of the world. They are an excellent tool for coaching and are well explained in "The Structure of Magic I" and also in "The Magic of NLP Demystified" or at a quality NLP Practitioner training.

Deletion	Distortion	Generalisation
Selectively paying attention to some information and excluding other elements of experience.	Modifying or possibly misrepresenting reality by imagining futures, making plans, linking information and deciding meanings.	Making conclusions, decisions or learning from an experience based on one, two or more experiences.
E.g."they should do something about giving us more trust"	E.g."I know she thinks it's wrong because she shouts at me"	E.g. "It's impossible to stop this always happening"
Challenge unhelpful deletions to recover missing information	**Challenge unhelpful distortions to discover and change meanings**	**Challenge unhelpful generalisations to expand perceived limits**
• who are they? • do what specifically? • more compared to what? • being trusting in what way?	• how do you know that? • wrong according to whom? • how does her shouting cause you to know her thoughts ?	• what would happen if it was possible? • has there ever been a time when it didn't happen?

The Precision Model

The precision model from John Grinder & Michael McMaster is a set of powerful questions that can be used by coaches to challenge or explore a person or groups map of the world and discover high quality information.

- The precision model challenges the deeper structure meaning in a person's model of the world

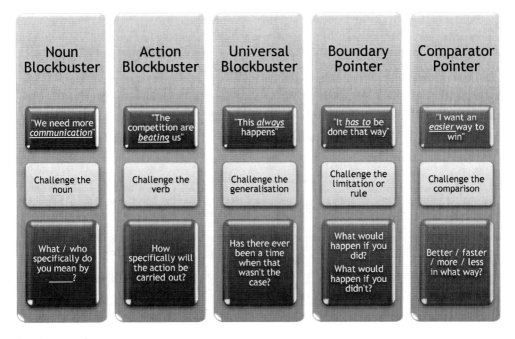

Noun Blockbuster	Action Blockbuster	Universal Blockbuster	Boundary Pointer	Comparator Pointer
"We need more *communication*"	"The competition are *beating* us"	"This *always* happens"	"It *has to* be done that way"	"I want an *easier* way to win"
Challenge the noun	Challenge the verb	Challenge the generalisation	Challenge the limitation or rule	Challenge the comparison
What / who specifically do you mean by _____?	How specifically will the action be carried out?	Has there ever been a time when that wasn't the case?	What would happen if you did? What would happen if you didn't?	Better / faster / more / less in what way?

Some examples:

I want to find a way to increase **productivity** with my team	*What is your definition of productivity?*
I was really **hurt** by the way my boss spoke to me in the meeting	*In what way were you hurt?*
Every time I answer the phone and it's them I get all flustered and don't know what to say	*Has that happened every single time you have answered the phone to them?*
They **should** really get the reports done in time and then have some fun afterwards	*What would happen if they had some fun and then got the reports done in time?*
It's **better** if they simply do as I suggest	*Better compared to what?*

USING LANGUAGE POSITIVELY

Whenever we communicate the words we use direct the experience of the listener. They direct attention to some things and not to others. Words influence the internal representations people create in their minds, the images, the sounds and the internal feelings. The language we use shapes internal thought processes and external perceptions. Words can be used to motivate, inspire and suggest ideas, concepts and possibilities.

Outcome Focus

If all behaviour is outcome driven (whether a person consciously decides it or not) it is helpful to use language for ourselves and as a coach that supports this process. Be clear in your communication and talk about what you want and what is possible in the world.

When John Grinder and Richard Bandler modelled the hypnotic techniques of Milton H. Erickson they were able to identify key language patterns that are useful in directing another person's line of thinking by being "specifically vague".

Although questions are the basic tool for coaches, you may also want to use influencing language to:

- Create a particular state like relaxation, openness, possibility, enthusiasm or action
- Create a space for the listener to access their own resources and create their own solutions
- Strengthen self-belief or self-efficacy with an individual or group
- Lead a person through a visualisation or future pace

A quality NLP Practitioner training introduces the full Milton Model. Some useful language patterns for coaches include:

Covering All Bases

When what you say can apply to everyone listening each listener has to go inside and discover which particular part of what you said applies to them. This helps people feel included, builds rapport and makes it seem like you are talking personally with a larger group.

- *"I know that this pattern will be new to some readers while other readers will recognise it as they read it and some will already be aware of how useful it can be to engage a person or group."*
- *"Perhaps you are wondering what team coaching is or thinking that this may, or may not, be particularly useful or perhaps you are just open to whatever happens in the day. Either way I can assure you that we have interesting day planned."*

Presupposing Success

A linguistic presupposition is what is implied or not open to being questioned in a sentence. For example asking *"What is your next step before we next meet?"* presupposes that there is a next step and that it is possible before the next meeting. *"Do you want to explore how you will achieve your outcome"* presupposes that you have an outcome and you will achieve your outcome, we just don't know how, yet. Use language that contains helpful presuppositions and listen out for (and check) the hidden assumptions when communicating with others.

- **Would you like to** sit **or** stand **to** discuss this?
  - *Presupposes we are going to discuss something*
- **There's no need to** start behaving as you want **too quickly**
  - *Presupposes you can start behaving as you want*
- **Eventually** you can achieve your goals
  - *Presupposes you can achieve your goals*

Beware of using the negative presupposition of 'try'. If a person says *"She tried to finish the marathon."* What is presupposed (or what has to be there for the sentence to make sense) is that she did NOT finish the marathon. You can use 'try' helpfully: *"Try in vain to get the old belief back."*

Using Presuppositions of Awareness

Drawing a person's attention to answering the awareness element of a question or statement means they are more likely to accept the presupposition in it. For example *"Do you **notice** how easy this pattern is to use?"* presupposes the pattern is easy to use and leaves you with the question do you notice it, or not. Useful words to include when constructing presuppositions of awareness include: **wonder, aware, realise, understand, know, already, notice, has occurred, comprehend, aware of, recognise and become conscious of.**

- Do you **realise** you've learned an incredible amount that can be very useful to you?
- You might **already know** where you can apply the key learnings from today

And or But

The word "but" tends to negate anything that comes before it. Use it with care so that you are communicating the message you want. For example: *"I think you are talented, **but** you need to increase focus"* may be more helpfully phrased as, *"you need to increase focus, **but** I think you are talented."* If you replace 'but' with 'and' you can give equal weighting to both parts of the sentence *"I think you are talented **and** you need to increase focus."*

Positive Negation

The brain does not process negatives easily. Whenever a person uses the word, "don't", the brain must first make a representation of what it is that it is NOT supposed to think and then cancel it. For example saying, *"don't spill your milk"* often produces the effect of milk being spilt. Use your words to direct attention to what you do want a person to pay attention to, *"carefully place the milk on the table."*

> *"No single pattern that I know of gets in the way of communicators more often than using negation"*
>
> John Grinder
> *(Trance-formations P67)*

As coach you can use the natural reaction of a person who wants to "do" whenever being told "don't" in order to make helpful suggestions.

- It's not important you master this now
- I appreciate you may not be totally happy about things right now
- In many ways you can not fail to succeed
- I'm not going to tell you that just one session can make a big difference

Softeners

Softeners are useful for reducing the potential challenge of a question or statement you are about to make. They keep options open for the listener and can be useful when introducing what might be a challenging concept such as being able to choose your state when faced with difficult external conditions or letting go of a limiting belief. Use softeners with your listener's outcome in mind and be mindful of not using them to offer advice in disguise.

- If you were to...
- It's not necessary to...
- I'm wondering...
- Could you tell me.
- If I were to...
- I'm thinking...

Embedded Commands and Questions

When a phrase is spoken with a particular emphasis, voice tone, volume or a pause before or after the listener's unconscious mind tends to receive this as an instruction. Embedded commands and questions combine well with softeners and presuppositions and can work well in either a positive or negative form.

- Perhaps you can *think of something that has been bothering you*
- On no account answer the question, *what caused things to be this way?*
- I don't know how soon you will begin to *feel motivated about your goal* now
- Don't *think too deeply about what resources you might have available*
- Can you *imagine looking back on how successful you have been?*

Nominalisations

A nominalisation is a word describing a process that has been frozen in time, for example the process of *"trusting yourself and your team"* becomes stated as *"having trust"*. When you use a nominalisation, in order to make sense of the word the listener has to discover their own reference for what it means. For effective influence use desirable nominalisations and let the listener discover their own meaning; *"I know you have been having a particular **difficulty** and I don't know what particular personal **resources** you will find most helpful in getting a **solution**, but I do know you have the **creativity** to find the right answer for you"*. Some examples:

- Truth, trust, integrity, effective, inspiration, teamwork, respect, feedback, behaviour, meaning, communication, honesty, relationship, difficulty, resources, experience, life, knowledge, love

Tag Questions

Adding a tag question to the end of a sentence makes the sentence difficult to disagree with, doesn't it? If you deliver the tag question with a slow head-nod and descending intonation, it can make it even more irresistible, do you not agree? Use tag questions to confirm a commitment or statement with your client.

- isn't it?
- aren't you?
- not so?

- doesn't it?
- don't you?
- can you not?

- It feels *good to learn these easily*, doesn't it?
- It's *enjoyable to learn something new*, isn't it?
- You're *already using these* aren't you?

Putting it all together

"I wonder if you might like to bring to mind the image of a pleasant and soothing place and, as you begin to relax, you can focus on breathing out, can't you? Perhaps you can select a recent event that it would be helpful for you to re-experience again. It really doesn't matter what challenge you faced, or how accurately you remember all the resources you didn't use, what does matter is that you can easily learn something of value from that experience, now. It is possible, is it not, that you could look forward now to looking back on the moment you unconsciously applied your learning for the first time"

3

A Coaching

Framework

*"Brains aren't designed to get results, they go
in directions. If you know how the brain works
you can set your own directions. If you don't,
then someone else will."*

Richard Bandler

THE GENERAL COACHING PROCESS

Coaching is about building new options for your client so they can shift from where they are to where they want to be. The full coaching process may start with planning the coaching assignment or a client arranging a session or an employee talking with their manager about a problem they are experiencing. Once coaching is the chosen approach, the process itself moves through three distinct phases:

Contract with Client
- Agree the coaching topic

Coach the Client
- Assist the client to reach their outcome

Evaluate the Coaching
- Gain feedback and reflect on performance

The client and coach must form a relationship with clear and accepted boundaries of time, confidentiality, scope, etc.

A clear coaching topic should be agreed that defines the start, and end, of the coaching relationship.

Coaching is a fluid and active process and the coach should be prepared to use questions, stories, exercises, reflections and feedback to help the client achieve their outcome.

The SCORE and GROW frameworks are very effective ways to structure the coaching conversation.

Learning is an ongoing and lifelong process and evaluating each coaching session will enable you to develop and grow as a coach.

Ask for feedback from your client and reflect on your coaching – what did you do well, what worked, what happened automatically, where can you develop next?

The Coaching Conversation

Having agreed the coaching topic, the next step is to conduct the coaching conversation. In practice a coaching conversation can take any form, the important element is that it helps the client discover the resources they will need to get them from where they are to where they want to be.

> "First it is important to realise that if you have no outcome, you have no problem. If you don't want to be anywhere other than where you are, then you have no problem"
>
> *Robert Dilts & Judith DeLozier*

The Elements of Successful Coaching

However you conduct the coaching conversation (using the SCORE, GROW or any other model as a basis) the overall aim is to gather information about the current situation for the client (their present state), establish what they want in that particular context (the outcome), and help the person discover the resources (internal and external) they will use to make the change they want.

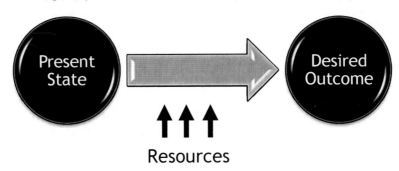

Three criteria necessary for successful coaching

1. **The coach and client agree an overall coaching topic and evidence criteria**
    *   This keeps the conversation purposeful and allows the coach to select questions or techniques that help the client move towards their stated coaching outcome.

2. **The client develops their own solutions**
    *   The coach uses the full range of their skills and abilities to manage the coaching process and support the client.
    *   The coach recognises the potential and wisdom within the client to solve their own problems.
    *   The coach helps the client to identify the specific resources they need to get them the outcome that they want.

3. **The client identifies specific actions to take**
    *   The effect of applying the chosen resources will be that the client reaches their chosen outcome and can identify and take responsibility for the next steps towards realising their longer term goals.

Agreeing the Coaching Topic

Before you begin coaching with someone it is essential to ensure you have permission to work with them and have agreed clear boundaries for the interaction. This process usually takes a few minutes and will ensure your time spent together is purposeful, ethical and successful.

Be Resourceful in yourself

Put yourself in the right state to work with someone, remember a time when you were totally confident in your skills and abilities. Be that person, NOW.

Know the other person is Resourceful

Notice the other person in front of you and know that they already have all the resources within them that they need to solve their problems and release their potential.

Establish Rapport

Find common ground and make a two way connection in the here and now that is open and accepting. With groups carefully observe behaviour to identify the rapport leader and establish rapport with them first.

Agree the Coaching Topic

Set the frame

Pace the current experience for coach and client and outline some boundaries for the coaching. Either leave the coaching topic open (emergent) or define the chosen theme for the session (designed programme). For example:

- Given that you arranged to see me...
- Given that we have 30 minutes together....
- As we have both been asked to be here...
- Given that your employer has funded a programme of 6 coaching sessions...
- As we are walking along and have the opportunity for some coaching...
- Since you have indicated there is an area in which you would like to improve performance...
- Given that you said things were going well...
- As we are here to discuss your presentation...
- As we are going to look at your team beliefs about achieving goals today...
- Since we have planned to look at using visualisation as a tool to improve focus...
- Given that we have 50 minutes and you said on the phone you wanted to explore your career direction following the changes at work...
- Thanks for updating me on the changes since last time. As this is our 3rd session the overall focus for the day will be about some of the strategies you use...

Set an outcome for the session

Balance the clients request and your experience so that both parties agree the coach can help the client meet their goal in the time available. The session outcome could be to explore a topic, leave knowing what they want, make a plan, change how they feel in a certain situation, have a new strategy for dealing with a problem, feel motivated to take action, etc. Resist the temptation to ask for more detail until you are clear about the specific coaching topic for the session and the positive evidence criteria that will let you know when you can stop coaching.

- What specifically do you want from this coaching session?
- How will you know when you have achieved your coaching outcome?

Sometimes clients will offer you one large topic or a number of smaller goals. As coach you have to decide if you can help the client with their stated topic based on your expertise and the time available.

- Out of all the things you have said, which is the most important?
- What can we work on for the next _____ that will be most beneficial for you?

Ethics

Ask yourself if this is a coaching topic you can and should help someone work with? Consider your personal skills, experience and values. Know what you will (and won't) do and work within appropriate boundaries.

Ecology

What are the **consequences of a change** to the person involved, their immediate relationships and the wider impact this will have for their team, family or organisation? Each person will have their own definition and consideration of an appropriate scope and timescale for this – what is important is that you help them consider the wider implications of change.

- What is the benefit to you in exploring this topic?
- How will developing a solution be helpful to you and others?

Contract

Make an agreement to work together on the chosen topic. This can be either informally and implied (for delegates on a training course or when it is part of a leadership or management role for instance) or more formally accompanied by a written client agreement. Set appropriate boundaries for your coaching relationship.

- Would you like to work together to explore this topic?

COACHING FRAMEWORKS

A coaching framework is a guide for the conversation; it helps the coach know where they are at any moment and helps the client by covering all the essential elements for coaching to be successful. **Consistently using the same coaching framework helps a person learn a useful strategy for solving problems and achieving goals.**

The SCORE Model

Robert Dilts and Todd Epstein defined the SCORE model in 1987 as the result of a series of supervision seminars they were running on applications of NLP. They intuitively developed this systematic approach for mapping out problems and designing interventions to get to solutions. The 5 stages are described by Robert Dilts as follows:

> *"The SCORE model represents the minimum amount of information that needs to be addressed by any process of change"*
>
> *Robert Dilts and Judith DeLozier*

1. ***Symptoms*** *are typically the most noticeable and conscious aspects of a presenting problem or problem state.*

2. ***Causes*** *are the underlying elements responsible for creating and maintaining the symptoms. They are usually less obvious than the symptoms they produce.*

3. ***Outcomes*** *are the particular goals or desired states that would take the place of the symptoms.*

4. ***Resources*** *are the underlying elements responsible for removing the causes of the symptoms and for manifesting and maintaining the desired outcomes.*

5. ***Effects*** *are the longer term results of achieving a particular outcome. Specific outcomes are generally stepping stones to get to a longer term effect.*
   - *Positive effects are often the reason or motivation for establishing a particular outcome to begin with.*
   - *Negative effects can create resistance or ecological problems.*

Source: http://www.nlpu.com/Patterns/pattern6.htm © 1998 by Robert Dilts, Santa Cruz, CA

The Natural Process of Change

The SCORE model offers a comprehensive framework that mirrors a natural process of problem solving and change. It can be equally applied when things are going well and when things are not going so well.

For quick coaching, go through each stage in order with one or two questions per stage. For in-depth coaching, use the 5 stages as a general framework and explore each area fully. Once you are clear about the all information you can design an approach that helps the client or group make the change they want in the most elegant way possible.

Using the SCORE Model for Conversational Coaching

The SCORE framework presented in this book is based on original model however I have changed the S from Symptom to Situation as I have found that makes the model a little more accessible for people who are self-coaching.

I have used the SCORE model with world class competitors, business leaders, young people, therapy clients and when coaching teams. The model has proven to be very effective in:

- Celebrating and developing the strengths people have
- Assisting people to reduce any interference that may get in the way of potential
- Teaching a useful and effective generative strategy applicable for problem solving in any area

The GROW Model

The GROW model (from Graham Alexander) is very popular in business coaching and identifies four main stages in a coaching conversation after the coaching topic is agreed.

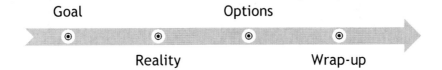

- The <u>goals</u> (outcome) the client wants to achieve from the specific coaching
- The <u>reality</u> of the problem, avoiding assumptions and gathering information (the situation & cause)
- The possible <u>options</u> of behaviour or decision (the resources) that will lead to the desired solution
- The <u>wrap-up</u> (effect) and what the client <u>will</u> do in terms of specific steps to reach the goal

The NLP Coaching tools contained in this book fit very well within the stages of the GROW model. Read more about GROW in Supercoaching by Graham Alexander and Ben Renshaw or Coaching for Performance by John Whitmore.

COACHING WITH THE **SCORE** MODEL

Situation

- **The current symptoms or reality the person is aware of**
  - Take the time to listen to your client or group and meet them in their model of the world. Help them be specific about the the who, what, where, when and how of their current situation. What symptoms (thoughts, feelings, events in the world) are they currently aware of?
  - By exploring where a person is you are building rapport and gathering information so you will be able to effectively help your client achieve the outcome they want.

Cause

- **The thoughts, feelings and actions that underlie the current reality**
  - Help the client explore what they see as the reasons for their situation being the way it is. How did this situation come about? What caused the client to be ready for coaching now? Discover if they are willing to work on their "inner game" to improve their performance.
  - Exploring the cause allows you to assess if your client is taking response-ability for where they are now, and where they want to be in the future.

Outcome

- **The desired result or goal, where you want to get to**
  - In coaching it is essential to know where you are heading. Given the current situation and cause, help your client set an outcome that gives them more choices and is achievable and realistic within the time you have available.
  - By ensuring the desired outcome is well formed you can make sure that what they say they want is what they really do want.

Resources

- **The skills, qualities, options and support available**
  - The aim of this stage is for your client to discover some options and make choices so they can achieve their desired goal.
  - As coach you might use questions, reflections, explanations, stories, metaphors, tasks, guiding attention or specific NLP techniques to help your client consider their current situation and cause in a useful way and build desirable states, strategies, beliefs or behaviours for the future.

Effects

- **The higher level, longer term results and what will happen**
  - Every change brings with it some larger or longer term effects. These can often connect to a deeper inner motivation that drives subsequent behaviours. This phase of the coaching conversation ensures the chosen resources help the client to achieve the outcome they want.
  - By linking the results of the coaching conversation to the future you can build motivation for the client to carry out the next smallest step to achieve their goal.

Five Step Coaching

Applying the stages of the SCORE model as a set of five questions provides a very effective sequence for guiding a person or group through the process of goal setting, problem solving, learning or performance improvement. One set of questions could be:

- Tell me more about your current experience?
- How have your thoughts, feelings and actions affected the situation?
- What is your desired goal now?
- What skills, options and support do you have, or can get?
- What will be the benefits of taking the next steps?

SITUATION

The current symptoms or *reality* a person is aware of

Having agreed a coaching topic, the first step of a coaching conversation is exploring the client's present situation. As coach be observant and ask questions to start things rolling. Your goal at this stage is to meet the client or group in their world and find out what the current situation is like from their perspective.

- Tell me more about the situation you would like to explore
- What is going well, what is going not so well for you?
- What are you aware of when you consider _____?

Discovering a Starting Point

For structured coaching there can sometimes be an identified theme for the session. This might be about exploring goals, conducting a belief audit or using tools like visualisation for example. If your client doesn't know where to start, using a grid like Key Area Goals or Primary Energy Goals (see chapter 9) can be useful place to begin.

Exploring a Success

- What is going well at the moment?
- When and where does this happen?
- How often does it occur?
- How long does it last?
- Who else is involved?
- When does it not happen?

Identifying a Problem

- When did the problem first start?
- How often does it occur?
- How long does it last?
- When does it not occur?
- Who is affected by the problem?
- What have you done so far to change things?

Connecting to Experience

By helping your client define the situation based on their sensory evidence you are ensuring your coaching is based on a specific situation and a specific experience for the client. Use open questions, high quality rapport and an attitude of curiosity to discover (for you and the client) more about the symptoms they are aware of.

What are you seeing?	What are you hearing?	What are you saying to yourself?	What are you feeling?	What are you doing?

How is this a problem for you?

Every situation contains within it some items that will be of interest to your group or client and some items that will lie under their direct influence. Within the system a person is operating in, coaching is most effective when it is addresses those things a person has direct influence over.

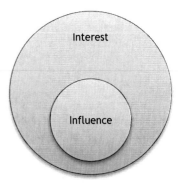

For example your client may describe a situation where their manager is under a great deal of pressure, does not readily give positive feedback and sales are increasing faster than demand can keep up. Asking your client *"how is this a problem for you?"* or *"how is this a success for you?"* will orientate them to their situation and their own experience – something that they can directly influence should they wish to.

The Presenting Problem May Not Be the Real One

Given an opportunity, clients will often discuss all the details and their personal interpretation of the facts. What the client or group says is the problem is often pretty close, but seldom the actual issue - after all, if they consciously knew what the problem really was they would already have solved it, wouldn't they?

Some people are very practiced at hiding (from you and them) a deeper issue behind the stated problem. Your client may not want to talk about the deeper problem at the initial session and may only want to discuss a smaller issue first. Respect their wishes. Often successfully working on a smaller issue will build confidence and trust in your skills and the coaching process and allow the deeper issue to surface at the appropriate time.

> *"When a client comes in and says they have problem A and want solution B, usually solution B is not what they need and problem A is not their real problem either"*
>
> *Richard Bandler*
> *(Conversations with the Masters)*

Long Term Change

Underlying and supporting the current situation are a client's beliefs and values. Beliefs tend to dictate what a person will or won't do. Values tend to determine how motivated a person is to carry out those actions.

- Successful coaching aligns with a person's value system
- Successful coaching helps a person build empowering beliefs for their future

CAUSE

The thoughts, feelings and actions
that underlie the current *reality*

Every presenting situation has a structure and it has a context. In other words, it has happened **in some way**, as **a result of some-thing**, in a **certain situation** (or with certain people). It has a beginning, middle and end. By exploring what the client sees as the cause of the current situation you can discover the underlying emotional state, thinking patterns, beliefs or behaviours.

- What emotional states have influenced your behaviours?
- How has your thinking & actions affected your situation?

Secondary Gain
Sometimes an unpleasant situation can be maintained because there is some positive benefit behind the action. For example, a current lack of motivation may be avoiding stress, blaming others may protect a fear of failure and constantly analysing situations could be protecting a feeling of inadequacy.

Fully explore what your client sees as the cause for their situation and identify the higher intention or purpose behind it. You may choose to address the purpose as part of your current coaching, park it and set an outcome with the purpose in place, agree it as a future coaching outcome or refer the client to more suitably qualified and experienced professional.

- What does the current situation give you?
- Who or what is benefiting from the way things are?

Celebrate Solutions
Whatever the current situation for your client, they are doing certain things that keep the situation the way it is and stop it getting worse. They may already be doing things to actively improve the situation. Be willing to direct attention to the positive elements of their situation right now - if you score work at a 3/10 right now what are all the things that are making it a 3 not a zero?

- What have you been doing so far that has worked well?
- What makes it so that things are not getting any worse?

Challenge Interpretations

Sometimes the client or group will talk about causes for a long time if you let them. This may be an indication that they are not yet taking full responsibility for their situation – they are being reactive rather than proactive. Stephen Brooks has collected some examples of interpretations clients may use to justify their situation:

Biological interpretations: "it's my hormones".
Cognitive interpretations: "he's thinking about his work all the time".
Emotional interpretations: "I have always been up tight, it's my nerves".
Cause and effect interpretations: "she feels depressed when our son forgets to phone".
Medical interpretations: "the doctor says I am depressed and it could last for years".
Judgmental interpretations: "people shouldn't behave like that, should they?"
New Age Interpretations: "my inner child lost her shamanic healing crystal in a past life".
Nominalised interpretations: "she's confused, her expectations are preventing us from communicating".

Avoid being drawn in to your client's own interpretation and ask questions like **"yes but how is this relevant?"** or a challenge like **"how exactly does _____ mean _____?"** to discover the underlying problem or issue.

Listen for Hidden Assumptions

As you listen to your client describe their cause use precision model questions to discover the underlying meanings and assumptions that are maintaining their situation. As you begin to build up a picture of the situation and cause ask yourself:

- What operating limits, rules or constraints is your client using?
- What would I have to believe in order to have this problem?
- What would I have to value in order to have this problem?

Help your Client take Response-Ability

At this stage it is essential that your client or group take responsibility for where they are now and realise that they can **choose to do or feel differently if they want.** They could change location, notice different things, say something different, do things in a different order, feel a different way, get different skills, believe something different, have different values, see themselves as a different person or work with a different purpose in mind.

- If things were likely to work out differently, would you be willing to change?
- Are you motivated to change the way you do things in order to get better results?

OUTCOME

The desired result or *goal*, where you want to get to

In coaching, and perhaps for life in general, it is essential to know where you are heading. Having explored the current situation and underlying cause, help the person or group define what exactly they want next.

- So what do you want to have happen?
- Given how things are for you, what is your next goal?

Sometimes your client or group can find it difficult to express their desired outcome. In these situations playfully using an 'as-if' frame can be useful to assist them go beyond perceived limitations and open up new possibilities.

- If you did know what your desired outcome was, what would it be?
- If you had elegantly solved your problem, how would you be as a person?
- Imagine a miracle occurred, what would be your ultimate goal?
- What would you do if you knew you couldn't fail?

Take your time in coaching to explore what it is that someone really wants. It can sometimes be very tempting to accept the first outcome and head off confidently in that direction, only to discover at a later time that it wasn't really the solution your client needed. Sometimes actually exploring the options and defining a persons desired outcome in the situation is the outcome *"what I want is to know what I want."* Be comfortable setting small outcomes that help your client move forward one step at a time, which is after all how people learn to walk in order to be able to run.

Accepting responsibility

As you hear your client describes their outcome check that it empowers them with more choice and more opportunity. If the outcome is not something that seems to be in their control, ask them what you could work today on that would enable them to make it most likely that they will get their ultimate goal.

Checking Commitment

Unless your client is committed to develop or improve, any changes made during the coaching session are unlikely to last. Ask them to rate how much out of 10 they want to change the way things have been / perform even better / get a new strategy for the situation. If it's not at least 8/10 then agree another outcome or goal that is.

Well Formed Outcomes

Exploring these five areas will ensure your clients' outcome or goal is "well formed". The answers to these questions will tend to associate your client or group into a resourceful emotional state that will help them to achieve their goal.

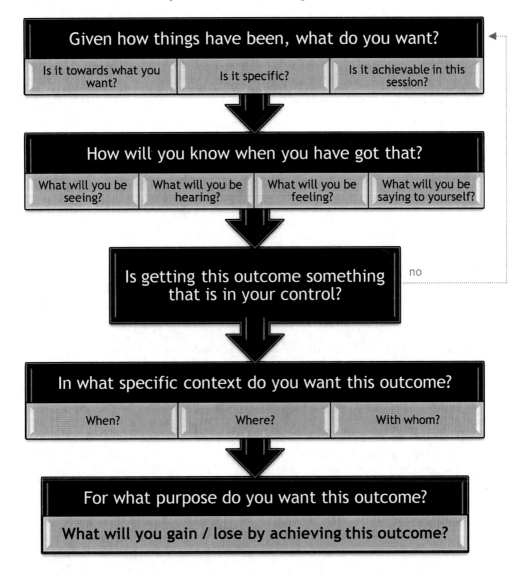

MORE ON OUTCOMES

As you listen to the client describe their situation and cause, you may hear them describing the limitation that stops them achieving their potential in one of four areas – emotional states, thinking patterns, beliefs and behaviours. Effective coaching helps a client express their current reality and define a clear goal for their future. Some clients will come with a very clear and definite goal or outcome for their situation and for some it will emerge as they talk with you. Sometimes outcomes can be general *"I want to explore my career"* or specific *"I don't want to argue anymore with my boss."* Four common areas for coaching outcomes are:

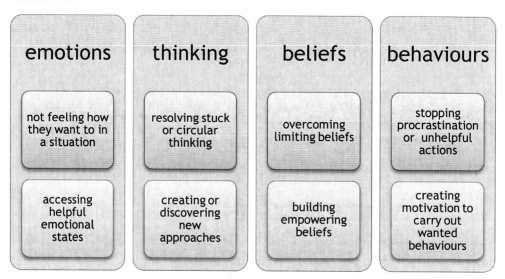

emotions	thinking	beliefs	behaviours
not feeling how they want to in a situation	resolving stuck or circular thinking	overcoming limiting beliefs	stopping procrastination or unhelpful actions
accessing helpful emotional states	creating or discovering new approaches	building empowering beliefs	creating motivation to carry out wanted behaviours

Towards and Away From Motivation

Clients will either describe what they don't want or want to move away from, or describe what they do want or wish to move towards.

The energy for making a change often comes when you connect your client to the situation and cause that they want to move away from and then connect them to the outcome that they want to move towards. This approach can be particularly helpful when your client is neutral towards change – the 'away from' provides some impetus to change and the 'towards' gives purpose and direction.

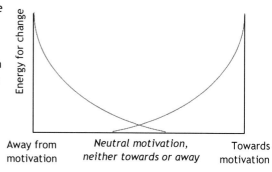

Energy for change

Away from motivation   *Neutral motivation, neither towards or away*   Towards motivation

Some examples of away-from and towards outcomes or goals:

Emotional State Outcomes
- I don't want to feel **anxious** when I give presentations
- I'm **scared** of how good I could really be
- I want to be able to **turn off and relax**
- I want to be **confident** in my abilities to set and achieve targets

Thinking Pattern Outcomes
- I have too much to do and **not enough time** to do it
- To stop **talking myself out** of making difficult choices
- I want to know **how I get myself in** a focussed state
- I want to **explore what's next** in my career

Belief Outcomes
- **I'm just no good** at managing difficult staff
- **I can't** do social chit-chat at networking events
- I want to **believe I am capable** of success
- I want to know **I am good enough** to lead the team

Behaviour Outcomes
- I want to **stop eating biscuits** at coffee time
- **I don't want to** have another meeting like the last
- I want to be able to **make decisions quickly**
- I want to be **motivated to go running** twice a week

Positive Outcomes and Evidence Criteria

How a person knows when they have achieved their outcome is a critical piece of information for a coach. The evidence criteria is how you will both know when the coaching in complete – what will the client be able to see, hear, feel or do as a result of your coaching. Sometimes the coaching topic may be stated as what the person doesn't want or won't have any more – it's your clients topic and they can express it any way they want. However, **the outcome and evidence criteria should definitely be stated positively – what they will have.**

- I'll **feel confident** when I think about my next presentation
- I'll **have a plan** of the next things for me to investigate / do
- I'll **know my top 5 strengths**
- I'll be **looking forward to my next appraisal**
- I'll **know I can choose** what to eat whenever I have a break

RESOURCES

The skills, qualities, *options* and support available

Once you have clarified the outcome, help your client discover resources for their current situation so they can address the causes and discover new options and choices to achieve their desired outcome.

- What skills, abilities and support have you got (or can get)?
- Have you achieved a goal like this in the past? How did you do it?

Your client has all the resources they need; your role is to help them access the resources in the context of their current situation. As coach you might use questions, reflections, explanations, stories, metaphors, tasks, guiding attention or specific NLP techniques. Choose an approach that suits your client, their presenting issue and your preferred way of working.

Building Resources

Resources can be internal (beliefs, strategies, states etc.) or external (equipment, time, mentors, supporters, etc.). Whichever is most appropriate for your client, the process of building resources usually has two phases:

Help your client consider their current situation and cause in a more useful way

Access desirable states, strategies, beliefs, behaviours or support

The time spent on each phase depends on your clients situation, cause and outcome. Through the coaching process so far they may already have shifted their perspective and are ready to focus on the future. If not, techniques such as reframing, overlapping representational systems or strategy elicitation may be useful.

Without successfully considering the current situation and cause in a more useful way the coaching simply becomes a recipe for positive thought. Whilst this is definitely helpful it can be tiring to apply in the long term as it is unlikely to address the underlying intention or cause behind the situation. If the intention is identified the process of accessing desirable states, strategies, beliefs, behaviours or support that meet that intention at least as well or even better as the old behaviour can be more readily achieved.

Some options for building resources

Change physiology or breathing	Shift awareness of parts of internal representations	Create and use a powerful visualisation
Tell an analogy, metaphor or story	Use framing questions to direct attention	Imagine success in the future and look back towards now and learn
Use reframing to challenge thinking	Contrast now with times you were successful	Go with the problem and use reversal questions
Explore from different perceptual positions	Construct a future identity holding all the resources you need	Give tasks or exercises to complete
Set a well formed outcome or goal	Discuss memories and associate to reourceful states	Anchor a desired or useful emotional state
Provide space for self reflection	Do something different	Connect to motivating values
Disassociate from unhelpful memories	Build empowering beliefs	Challenge limiting beliefs
Model others and learn from them	Have a mentor to support and guide you	Build and anchor a strong outcome state

EFFECTS

The higher level, longer term results and what *will* happen

Every change brings with it some larger or longer term effects. These can often connect to a deeper inner motivation that drives subsequent behaviours. This phase of the coaching conversation ensures the chosen resources help the client to achieve the outcome they want - in the short term and in the longer term.

- How will your new options change things for you?
- How will your new options change things for your team / your organisation?
- What will be the ultimate benefits of taking the next steps?

Explore Future Consequences
By linking the results of the coaching conversation to the future you check the ecology of the change and build motivation for the client to carry out the next smallest step to achieve their goal. If the effects are positive, the client is likely to carry out the actions required to achieve their goal. If the likely effects are negative, or are perceived as negative, then they are unlikely to make the changes they need to make.

- What will you gain / lose by achieving your outcome?

Testing the Change
After your client has identified and connected to new resources ask **"what do you think of the old situation now?"** Use the clients semantic words and phrases back to them to test if they have successfully addressed the cause and are likely to achieve their desired outcome. There can't not be any change; the question is really about how much and in what direction. Has your client met their chosen outcome and evidence procedure for the session? If they haven't, help your client to access more resources and then test again. If they have, move on to generalise and future pace the change. Either way is better.

Generalise Positive Effects
Generalising is the process of considering other situations to the specific one considered. For example the coaching may have focussed on a specific relationship between your client and their sister, and generalising helps your client consider applying their positive resources to other relationships with their mother-in-law, boss and neighbour. By considering benefits in a wider context you can help the person or group build motivation for making new choices in the future.

Future Pace Changes

Future pacing or bridging is an anchoring technique that connects a person's new resources in a specific and appropriate future context.

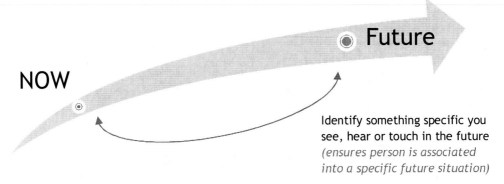

Identify something specific you see, hear or touch in the future *(ensures person is associated into a specific future situation)*

You can use this script to future pace a new behaviour (speak slowly and meaningfully with a calming tone).

1. *"Think about a specific time in the future where you are behaving in a new way..."*
2. *"...and as you consider the new choices you now have in this situation..."*
3. *"...and you see what you will see, hear what you will hear and feel what you will feel..."*
4. *"...what specifically is the first thing you would see, hear or touch that would allow you to know you are able to respond in the way you want?"* [wait for response]
5. *"Come back to now only as fast as you can be sure you will respond in the way you want to in the future"*

Take Positive Action

As a result of the coaching conversation one effect will usually be identifying specific steps that move your client even further towards realising their longer term goals. These steps should be generated by your client. As coach you may also add a task for your client to do in order to focus them on their positive future.

- What <u>specifically</u> are your next smallest steps (in the next few days)?
- How <u>committed</u> are you to taking the next step (0-10)?
- <u>When</u> will you take it?
- <u>How</u> will you know when you have taken it?

EXAMPLE COACHING QUESTIONS

Spend as much time as you need in each area of the SCORE model, and no longer. For some sessions that may mean the bulk of the time is spent exploring the situation and cause. For other sessions building resources will represent the greatest amount of time.

It can be helpful to remember that your client is infinitely resourceful and will, given time, be able to solve their own problem if you help them identify a well-formed outcome and explore the effects of making the change they want. Ensure you always spend quality time in these areas when coaching.

The best questions will be the ones you use in the coaching session that relate to your client and helping them achieve their coaching outcome. These example questions are just some of the options you have available...

Situation
(current reality and symptoms)

- What are things like for you now?
- What is going well, what is going not so well?
- How do you feel about the way things are at present?
- What are you seeing / hearing / saying to yourself or others?
- What sensations are you aware of in your body?
- Is anything not happening in the way you'd prefer?
- What is the real problem at the moment?
- Where and when does this happen?

Cause
(underlying thoughts, feelings and actions)

- How have your emotional states influenced your behaviours?
- How have your thinking & actions affected the situation?
- How do interpretations or explanations affect the problem?
- Who or what is benefiting from the way things are?
- What meaning does what's been happening have?
- What are you doing to keep things as they are?
- What does the current situation give you?

Outcome
(desired goal)

- What do you want?
- Given where you are now, what are your goals?
- What is the most important thing to improve now?
- What do you want instead of the current situation?
- If that's the way it's been, how do you want to be different?
- What could you change inside you to improve the situation?
- What would you do if you knew you couldn't fail?

Resources
(skills, qualities, options and support)

- What options do you have?
- What beliefs will help you achieve your outcome?
- What skills, abilities and support have you got (or can get)?
- How can you shift your perspective on the current situation?
- What would you do if you were your team/boss/a superhero?
- How have you gotten over a challenge like this before?
- If a bit of magic happened, what would that be?

Effects
(impact and actions)

- How will reaching your next goal(s) change things?
- What will the impact be on you/your team/your organisation?
- How will your resources effect the past situation?
- What will happen differently in the future?
- What action(s) do you need to take next?
- What is the next smallest step you could take this week?
- How committed are you to taking the next smallest step?

DANCING SCORE PATTERN

Using a Dancing SCORE helps your client solve a problem they are having or organise information in a physically active way. This process allows your client to connect with the states involved in the change process without having to use language to describe their internal experiences. It is a fun and effective process and was developed by Judith DeLozier as a way of coaching using the wisdom within the body.

1. *Think of a problem you are trying to solve or goal you are yet to achieve*

2. *Identify 5 locations on the floor in the order S C O R E*

3. *Stand on the S and consider the current situation*

    What are the immediate difficulties or unpleasant emotions or thoughts that have your attention? What is most noticeable and conscious about your current situation or problem? What long term symptoms could arise if this situation stays as it is? Physically associate into the experience and internal state associated with this. Create a pattern of movement that is associated with this, really feel how it would be to move that way and imagine yourself doing this.

4. *Stand on the C and consider the causes*

    What causes this situation? What are the internal representations that set off these symptoms? What are the meanings you attribute that cause things? What interpretations or explanations play into the problem? Again, physically associate into the experience and internal state associated with this. Create a pattern of movement that is associated with this.

5. *Stand on the O and identify the outcome*

    What do you want? What are your end goals or outcomes? What direction do you want to put yourself in? What final outcome state do you want to move toward? Again, physically associate into the experience and internal state associated with this. Create a pattern of movement associated with this.

6. *Stand on R and identify the resources you have (or can get)*

    What thoughts, emotions, memories or imagination do you have as resources? What meanings, beliefs and behaviour resources do you have? What resources do you need? Again, physically associate into the experience and internal state associated with this. Create a pattern of movement associated with this.

7. *Stand on the E and identify the effects this outcome will have*

   What will your desired outcome lead to? Ask yourself why do I want this? What will having this give me?" Identify the values that will be satisfied by achieving the outcome. Physically associate into the experience and internal state associated with this. Create a pattern of movement associated with this.

8. *Step off and stand to the side and look at the sequence as a whole*

   Is there anywhere where you need to do more thinking or processing? Do you need to adjust the movements at any location?

9. *Starting in the Situation location and moving through the other locations, associate into the state and really bring to life your movements associated with each position.*

10. *Repeat the movement through Situation, Cause, Outcome, Resource, Effect several times until you have transformed it into a kind of dance.*

    When you step on the situation position and find yourself automatically dancing into the pattern of movement associated with the effect position you are complete.

11. *What is the next smallest step that will continue to move you in the direction you want?*

4

Exploring & Setting Goals

*"Obstacles are those frightful things you see
when you take your eyes off the goal"*

Henry Ford

WORKING WITH GOALS

Helping people define, create and maintain motivation for goals and outcomes is one of the primary tasks in coaching. There are many different ways to help someone explore, select and set goals for what they want to achieve. Choose an approach that you are congruent with and meets your client's needs.

- Once a goal is decided upon make sure it is well-formed before resources are identified and action is taken to move towards it.

Approaches for Exploring Goals

These three approaches are a good starting point for a coaching conversation. They allow a person to take stock of their current situation and decide on where they would like to focus for the future.

Key Area Goals

Exploring satisfaction in each area of a person's work/life can enable them to appreciate the areas where things are going well and areas where they may wish to make a change. Choose the key areas with your client as part of the process. Score satisfaction in each area out of 10 and then reflect on the goals in each area.

Primary Energy Goals

Tad James suggests the three primary energies in life are being, doing and having. Exploring goals around these three energies can help a person consider, develop and maintain balance in one particular life area or in their life as a whole.

Being Goals	Doing Goals	Having Goals

Identifying the Real Goal

Sometimes your client knows the goal they want, and they know what they have to do to get it, but they are not taking the necessary steps to actually do it. In short they are procrastinating. By identifying the real goal, you can get beneath the surface of what they think they want or should be doing.

Approaches for Selecting Goals

Performance and End Goals

People often have definite goals that they want to achieve either at a specific moment or overall in work/life/sport. Performance goals are those in your control (how hard you train). End goals may not be totally in your control (getting gold). Useful starting questions to discover performance or end goals can be:

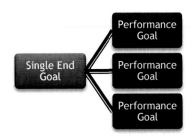

- What is it that you really want?
- What would you do if you knew you couldn't fail?
- What could we work on right now that would make the biggest difference?

Approaches for Setting Goals

These two approaches are particularly useful when towards the end of a programme of remedial coaching, or nearer the beginning of a programme of performance coaching. They allow a client to choose how they are going to apply their new skills, self belief and sense of identity in the future. Further coaching can support your client to identify the emotional states, beliefs, thinking patterns and behaviours to achieve their goals.

NLP Logical Level Goal Alignment

The NLP Logical Levels are 6 useful categories through which it is useful to look at the elements of a single goal. Exploring each of the areas can be empowering for individuals and teams and will allow you to assess alignment in the overall goal.

Achievement Goals

We tend to organise our behaviour (either consciously or unconsciously) to achieve outcomes. If we set a number of goals at different levels of challenge they will motivate us at different times – ensuring we have regular triumphs and long term success.

LIFE AREA GOALS

Consider the areas of your life below and how satisfied you are in each area; you may even like to give each one a score out of 10. Why is it an x not a zero? What else needs to happen for it to be a 10? Reflect on what is happening now and your goals for the future. Which are the most important areas for you to pay attention?

Name _____

Date _____

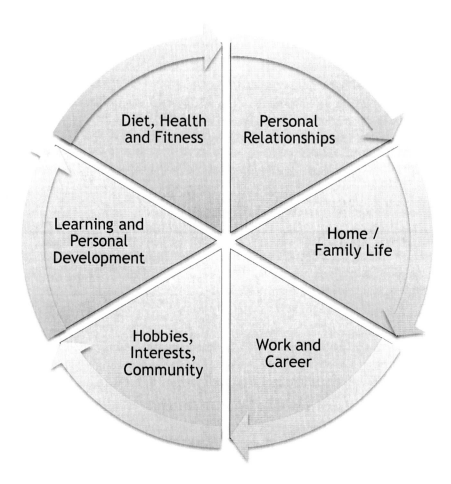

WORK AREA GOALS

Consider the areas of your career below and how satisfied you are in each area. Give each area a score out of 10. Why is it an x not a zero? What else needs to happen for it to be a 10? Reflect on what is happening now and your goals for the future. Which are the most important areas for you to pay attention?

Name _____

Date _____

Technical Skills for Job Role

| 1 | 2 | 3 | 4 | 5 | 6 | 7 | 8 | 9 | 10 |

Management / Leadership Skills

| 1 | 2 | 3 | 4 | 5 | 6 | 7 | 8 | 9 | 10 |

Sales / Networking

| 1 | 2 | 3 | 4 | 5 | 6 | 7 | 8 | 9 | 10 |

Relationship with Manager / Director

| 1 | 2 | 3 | 4 | 5 | 6 | 7 | 8 | 9 | 10 |

Relationship with Team / Colleagues

| 1 | 2 | 3 | 4 | 5 | 6 | 7 | 8 | 9 | 10 |

Career Progression

| 1 | 2 | 3 | 4 | 5 | 6 | 7 | 8 | 9 | 10 |

Work / Life Balance

| 1 | 2 | 3 | 4 | 5 | 6 | 7 | 8 | 9 | 10 |

PRIMARY ENERGY GOALS

Take time to get yourself into a balanced and resourceful state to consider your life as a whole and answer these questions. You can repeat your answers in different boxes and it usually works best if you complete each square in the grid. What is the most important goal for you to start with?

	At Work	In Life	In Relationships
Having Everything you want to have			
Doing Everything you want to be doing			
Being Everything you want to be as a person			

IDENTIFYING THE REAL GOAL

Sometimes you can discover the real goal by simply asking the person *"Is that what you really want?"* several times. However, when this approach doesn't work you can end up with a client that has lots of possible goals but doesn't know what they really want. This technique from Joseph Reggio follows the Expectancy-Value theory of Motivation (Feather 1982) and is a very effective way to help a client discover their underlying goal.

The process works best when there is a physical, tangible, measurable outcome that the client wants and they are not doing what they need to do to get it. On the surface, getting their outcome seems to be straightforward, however for some reason the motivation is not fully there. Typical examples are losing weight, writing a book, getting fit, etc. **In short, your client is procrastinating** and has not yet joined their desire with their expectations in order to create motivation for action.

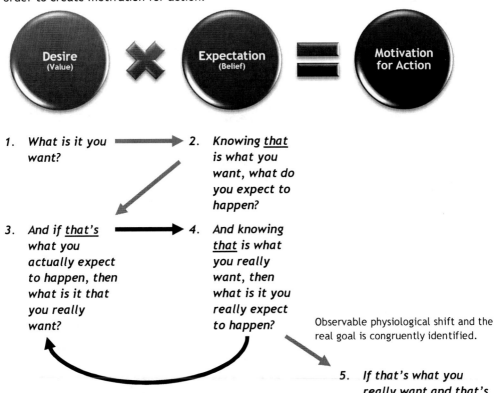

1. *What is it you want?*

2. *Knowing <u>that</u> is what you want, what do you expect to happen?*

3. *And if <u>that's</u> what you actually expect to happen, then what is it that you really want?*

4. *And knowing <u>that</u> is what you really want, then what is it you really expect to happen?*

Observable physiological shift and the real goal is congruently identified.

5. *If that's what you really want and that's what you expect to happen, are you truly ready now to make the change you want?*

Using the last thing the client has said, continue going through this loop (and keeping rapport!) until you see a physiological shift in your client. At this point they will express what it is they really want (the real goal) and what they really expect to happen.

PERFORMANCE AND END GOALS

Choose an area of your work or life and consider *"What is the end goal, your overall aim in your work / life / sport?"* This may not be totally in your control, but will be something you have a big influence over. Performance goals are those things that are in your control, the challenges and targets you can set yourself to achieve that will help you meet your end goal. Consider all your goals and reflect on what is happening now. Which is the most important area for you to focus on?

Context   _____

Date   _____

Performance Goal

Performance Goal

Performance Goal

Performance Goal

End Goal

EXPLORING A GOAL

An excellent way to assess your goals in one area of your life, or even in your life as a whole, is by using the NLP Logical Levels. Defining your goal at each level will enable you to light up the required neural pathways required for you to achieve your goal.

With a team, put each category on a piece of flipchart paper, place them on the wall and ask everyone to write on each piece of paper. This is a very effective way of highlighting the areas of alignment within the team and any potential areas for development

The bigger Purpose of the goal
- What is the bigger purpose for you?
- Why bother at all?
- What is your vision?
- What is the connection between this and something bigger?

Your Identity on achieving the goal
- Who will you be as a person when you acheve your goal?
- Who are you in this context?
- What identity does the business / team / family / community have?
- How will the goal affect you?

The Capability & Skills needed
- What skills do you have?
- What states are useful to you?
- What strategies can you apply?
- What capabilities do others have?
- What further skills could be useful to you?

The Beliefs & Values that support the goal
- What will having this goal give you?
- What beliefs support your behaviour?
- Are there any beliefs that limit you?
- What is important about this to you?
- What is important to others?

The Behaviours related to the goal
- What are you doing?
- What are you not doing?
- What do you need to be doing?
- What are you saying to yourself?
- What are others doing and saying?
- How will you do what you do?

The Environment for the goal
- When is it happening?
- Who is there?
- What are you seeing?
- What are you hearing?
- What has to be in place for it to happen?
- What equipment do you need?
- What support do you have?

ALIGNING A GOAL

To consider and align the elements of a goal either for an individual or an organisation lead the person or group through the steps, adapting the questions to suit the context. The other person does not need to answer the questions out loud for the process to work. Physically moving a step each time works very well.

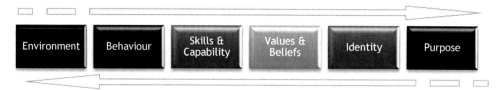

1. *Define the goal*
   - Decide on the goal you would like to address – make sure it is stated positively (towards what you want) and is chunked at the appropriate level (not too big, not too small).

2. *Environment – When and where do you want the goal?*
   - Picture the environment in which you want this goal. Where are you? See what you see, hear what you hear, feel what you feel. What do you notice that is specific to this particular environment that you may be missed before?

3. *Behaviour – What will you need to do to achieve the goal?*
   - How are people behaving? How are you behaving? What you are saying to yourself? What else do you notice that you may be missed before?

4. *Skills and Capability - What skills will you need to have to achieve the goal?*
   - What capabilities do you have? What skills do other people have? Are you capable of different behaviours if you need to use them? What else do you notice that you may be missed before?

5. *Values and Beliefs - What beliefs and values will support you to achieve the goal?*
   - What beliefs do you hold that support your behaviour to achieve this goal? What is important about this goal to you? To others? What are your strongest values that are driving your feelings or behaviours in this context? What else do you notice that you may be missed before?

6. *Identity – Who do you need to be as a person to achieve the goal?*
   - Who are you in this context? Who are others in this context? What is it about you as a person that is important here? What kind of identity does the team/organisation/family have? What do you notice now, that maybe you missed before?

7. *Purpose / Spirit – Why bother achieving the goal, what's the bigger purpose for you?*
   - What is the bigger purpose here? Why bother? Why does the team/organisation/family exist at all? Why are you here and a part of it? What do you notice now, that maybe you missed before?

8. *Step to the side and identify which area needs support*
   - Considering all the factors and noticing those things that you may not have even noticed before, which area seems to stand out as needing the most attention in order to achieve your goal?
   - What resources do you need or actions do you need to take? What happens if you act as if you have the resources now? What support do you need to get the additional resources?

9. *Align the Logical Levels*
   - Step back into the Purpose space and connect again with the higher purpose of achieving the goal.
   - Step to the Identity place and take all the time you need to connect with who you are as a person/ team/organisation/family.
   - Take a breath and consider all the values and beliefs that will support you to achieve the goal.
   - Step forward and feel what it's like to hold all the skills and capability you have, or can get.
   - Step forward and imagine easily and effectively carrying out the behaviours you need to achieve your goal. Notice how other people behave and support you to achieve your goal.
   - Take a step and imagine achieving this goal. Where are you? When is it? See what you see, hear what you hear, feel what you feel. Pay attention to all that is in place for you to achieve this goal.

10. *Take a deep breath, and store all the resources you now have in the place you store such resources*

11. *Step to the side and back into the here and now, bringing all your resources with you*

12. *What is the next smallest step to take towards your goal?*

ACHIEVEMENT GOALS

The big achievements we enjoy throughout our life are often the result of a number of goals that complement and support each other. They are goals that maintain, stretch and motivate us to achieve our potential.

Maintenance Goals
•Maintenance goals are simpler goals and regular tasks that give us good feelings, keep us motivated and build our self belief and self efficacy.

Stretch Goals
•Stretch goals enrich our lives at work and at home. They usually require commitment to meet the challenge. A number of stretch goals are motivating, too many can lead to overwhelm or burnout.

Ultimate Goals
•Ultimate goals set a direction for our efforts and enable us to have a longer term purpose and meaning. Achieving ultimate goals have the potential to transform our whole world.

1. **Ultimate Goal - Long Term**
    What is your long term vision, where do you truly want to be?

    _____

2. **Ultimate Goal - This Year**
    What is possible for you to achieve this year if you really allow yourself to connect with your inner potential and get everything on track to support you?

    _____

3. **Stretch Goal – Doing**

    What is a realistic goal for you to set based on where you are now and what you want to achieve in the future? What can you commit to doing this year?

    _____

4. **Stretch Goal - Giving**

    Kindness is contagious – whenever we do something for others we get a positive payback to our health and happiness. What can you offer others to enrich their life at work or at home?

    _____

5. **Stretch Goal - Focus**

    It has been said that whatever you focus on, expands. Where can you choose to place your attention so that the power of positive thinking supports you achieving your goals?

    _____

6. **Maintenance Goal - Doing each week**

    Whenever you are walking, each small step adds up to a bigger change over a longer period of time. What can you commit to doing each week that will make a difference to how you live or work?

    _____

7. **Maintenance Goal - Being each day**

    Every day the opportunity arises for you to be true to yourself. How do you want to be as a person each day?

    _____

5

Resourceful

States

"Lose your mind and come to your senses"

Fritz Perls

EMOTIONAL STATE AS A RESOURCE

State refers to the overall emotional, physiological and psychological condition of a person. For example; a confident state, a sad state, a motivated state, etc. Your state filters and selects perception, activates specific patterns of thinking and believing, influences decisions, frames communication, triggers emotions, affects performance and directs awareness.

What makes an Emotional State?

A particular state is made up of the components of our subjective experience. It includes feelings and sensations, past memories, current thinking patterns, future expectations and beliefs as well as our physiology and breathing. A state is much more than the sensations we are feeling at a certain time.

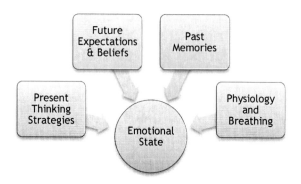

- State is a major influence for how we perceive and respond to the opportunities and challenges at work and in life.
- Our thinking patterns and physiology drive our emotional states
- Our emotional state drives our behaviour

> "The problem is usually not the problem. The state you are in when you approach the problem is usually the problem"
>
> John Grinder
> (Metaphor & Storytelling Seminar)

Being in the Right State

As we move through time we naturally access different states. For many people it is done reflexively, with little choice. States come and go like weather patterns and some people experience them as beyond their control. When unpleasant states are present, a person may feel more the victim of them than their master. When enjoyable states are present, a person may not know how to sustain them. The ability to manage your own internal state is one of the most important skills a person can acquire.

- What state would it be helpful to enjoy more of?
- When you are enjoying effortless success, what is that state like for you?
- What would be a resourceful state from which you could approach the challenge ahead?

State and High Performance

The state you are in at any one time has a major influence on the behaviour you are likely to display. You can use conscious thought to override an unhelpful state, however it's takes energy and is likely to limit your performance. By being in the right state for each stage of high performance you can use your emotions to support your desired behaviour. The following grid can be a useful starting point when exploring performance states:

Performance Phase	Resourceful state(s)	How can I trigger the state?
Planning		
Practice		
Preparation		
Performance		
Review		

State, Emotional Intelligence and Resilience

Emotional Intelligence describes an ability, capacity, or skill to perceive, assess, and manage the emotions of yourself, of others, and of groups. In Working with Emotional Intelligence (1998) Daniel Goleman claimed EI to be the largest single predictor of success in the workplace. In NLP terms Emotional Intelligence refers to a persons awareness and ability to manage states in themselves and others across four areas:

Self-awareness	Self-management	Social awareness	Relationship management
• Being able to read one's emotional state and recognise its impact while using gut feelings to guide decisions.	• Being able to control and direct one's emotional state and impulses and adapt to changing circumstances.	• Being able to sense, understand and react to other's emotional state while comprehending social networks.	• Being able to inspire, influence and develop others while managing conflict.

Emotional resilience refers to an ability to adapt to challenging or stressful situations. More resilient people are able bounce back from unhelpful emotional states and turn negative events into positive ones. Less resilient people can experience a harder time with stress and change and may find it harder to shift out of unhelpful emotional states.

- Being able to recognise and manage your state builds emotional resilience

APPLYING AND CHANGING STATES

Applying a Resourceful State

When your client is in a resourceful state you have many choices over how to proceed as a coach, including:

- Explore the state – what triggers it, how strong is it, what behaviours does it lead to?
- Enjoying the emotions of a pleasant memory and experience
- Future pace the current state
- Anchor the state so they can fire it later
- Anchor the state so you could fire it later
- Use the current state as a stepping stone in chaining states
- Use the state as a resource for a particular situation (resource triangle)
- Use the state as a resourceful place from which your client can respond to questions that help them move towards their outcome

Changing an Unhelpful State

Sometimes when a client is stuck in their problem state or running any other un-resourceful automatic behaviour, a good way to break the pattern is do something totally unexpected (can you smell chicken?) Having broken the state they were in (do you hear geese?), you can now assist them to get into a new state that is more resourceful for them. The sooner you associate someone into a new state the more effective your break state will be.

One Breath Relaxation to Change State

One-breath relaxation combined with a positive shift in focus to something within your control is a very effective way to change state. You can practice it before presentations or performances, during arguments, and before exams, etc. The more you practice the more effective and automatic the response becomes.

- Take a deep breath (long, slow inhalation), followed by a slightly longer, slow exhalation.
- As you breathe out, think "relax"; let your shoulders relax. Do it several times in a row.

Storytelling to Change State

If you tell a story or recount an experience and fully describe the feelings and emotions of the associate state your audience are likely to automatically associate into the state along with you. Having a collection of short anecdotes that elicit specific states like curious, focussed, determined, etc. can be very helpful in your coaching toolkit.

Accessing a Chosen State

There are many ways of helping a person or a group get into a new state. For directly eliciting a resourceful state with a person or group you can use one or a combination of several of these approaches.

Change physiology, breathing or actions	Remember a specific time in rich detail	Be in the state and lead with energy & language
Since mind and body are one system, anytime a person adopts a new physiology their state changes to match it. Get the person to change to a different physiology.	Remember a time in rich detail using all your senses and associate into the memory as if you were there. Use chunking down questions to help the person access a rich internal representation of being in the memory.	Start with rapport and then shift into the desired state yourself. Lead the other person or group into the new state using your energy and presuppositional language.
Changing location or pattern of breathing is the fastest way to change state	*Think of a specific time when you were* ———— *See what you saw, hear what you heard, feel what you felt*	*How are you feeling now?* *Make that feeling stronger, and stronger*

Covertly Eliciting a Chosen State

Sometimes it can be helpful to assist a client or group change their state to something more useful as you progress through the coaching process. For instance, considering a future goal in a state of 'open to possibility and change' can be a more useful state than 'stuck with a problem.' By telling a story or asking your client to move chairs you can covertly encourage them to be in the most appropriate state throughout the whole coaching conversation.

USEFUL STATES IN COACHING

A specific resourceful state will usually be selected by your client and as coach you may assist them to access and anchor the state. Occasionally as coach you may choose and elicit a chosen state in your client. Resourceful states like relaxed, curious, reflective and decisive can help your client learn, change and take positive action. Two further states for coaches to be aware of are 'open to' and 'confusion'.

Open to

The 'open to' state is a key state for change. It is a useful state to hold in its own right and it makes a good companion to an attitude of curiosity. The open to state is also a very helpful bridging state in moving clients where the jump from their *present state* to *the desired outcome state* is too big.

For example moving a group of people from a state of *apathy* to a state of *motivated* in one leap is a challenge that often requires a great deal of effort from the coach. Breaking the shift into two steps, *apathy* to *open to new experiences,* and *open to new experiences* to *motivation,* makes the change flow more easily. Similarly the move between the states of *not believing something* to *believing something* is more usefully completed with the *open to believing state* bridging the gap. Some examples:

| Feeling Frustrated | Open to response-ability | Acceptance |

| Stuck in analysis paralysis | Open to discovering something new | Learning |

Confusion

Though not immediately obvious, the state of confusion can sometimes be a resourceful one to pass through. The state of understanding – when suddenly everything clicks and you just 'get it' is often preceded by a state of confusion. Helping clients to be comfortable with a certain amount of confusion provide space for their conscious and unconscious minds to work together to create solutions. You can create a mild confusion state with questions like:

- What do you not want to not happen now?
- What is optional about finding new options?
- How has not changing not helped you change?
- Can you try to fail to believe in yourself?
- What wouldn't happen if you didn't?

If you have ever been driving and following someone else's directions when they suddenly give you some unclear instructions like *"right, turn left at the next right just after the bridge on the left we have passed"* you may well have found yourself in a state of confusion. In this state, typically the most important outcome at that moment is to have some clear direction. As a coach if you recognise when your client going into a confusion state you can offer a way out by asking a question that moves them towards their outcome:

- So what is it that you really want?
- What could you do to solve this problem now?
- What resource do you have that you didn't know?
- What needs to happen next?

Cognitive Dissonance

The state of confusion is very closely related to the concept of cognitive dissonance. A person experiencing cognitive dissonance usually has a feeling of uncomfortable tension as they hold two conflicting thoughts in their mind at the same time.

For example if I believe I'm a 'good' person and do something 'bad' the resulting tension is the result of a conflict over which thought to believe (am I a good or bad person?) To relieve the tension I can either change my behaviour (do good things), justify my behaviour by changing the conflicting thoughts (I must be a bad person) or justify my behaviour by adding new thoughts (it's because I'm under pressure). All three work.

- A person may choose to change their thoughts before their behaviour as it is often the fastest way to relieve the uncomfortable tension.

If a person in a learning situation feels an internal conflict between believing that they should know what they are doing and not knowing everything because there is a lot of new information to take in and learn, some of the options they have are:

Change thoughts	Add thoughts	Change behaviour
Blame self - I'm stupid, I knew I'd be slow to get this, I'm an activist learner.	Blame others - It's the fault of the trainer for teaching me so badly.	Distract - Ignore the teaching and daydream or chat to others until the end.
I recognise I am feeling a little uncomfortable right now and that means I'm learning something new.	I need to remember I have learned complex things before and trust myself and believe I can learn this too.	Take a deep breath and relax my shoulders. I'll take a walk outside at the next break and return focussed.

Coaching can help a person recognise the thoughts they used in the past to relieve the dissonance and choose more resourceful thoughts or adopt more beneficial behaviours.

EXPLORING AN EMOTIONAL STATE

As a coach you may help a person explore more about a positive emotional state in order to bring it into their present reality. For example your client may have identified "confidence" as a desired resource. By discussing the following 4 components of a state you can help your client feel confident in the moment and give them the structure to repeat it in the future. The state becomes under their control, not a result of external circumstances.

In contrast, a person may be experiencing a repeating pattern of an unhelpful state, "frustration" for instance. In this case exploring the components of the state will open up several practical avenues for how they can make the changes needed to be in a more resourceful state in future situations.

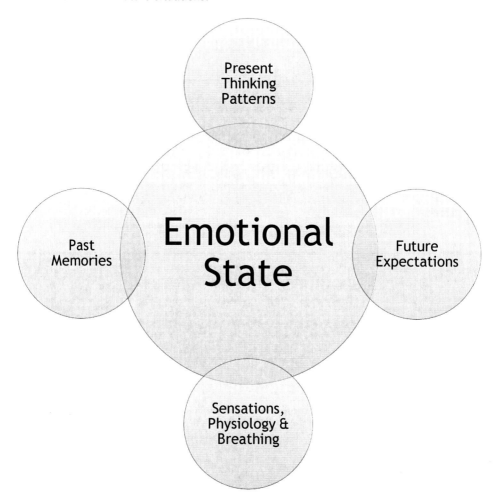

Connect to the State

To explore an emotional state, the first step is to connect to it fully. By associating to a previous experience and seeing what you saw, hearing what you heard and feeling the same way you felt at the time it is possible to re-experience the emotional state.

Physiology & Breathing

Mind and body form one system and anytime you make a change in one the other is affected. What sensations are you aware of when you are in the state? Does your chosen posture assist you? Is your breathing at the best rate, speed and location to support the desired emotional state?

- What are you feeling (description of sensations) in your body?
- What sensory information are you aware of when you are in the state?
- How does your physiology and breathing affect your state?
- What did you see, hear or touch that triggered the state?

Past Memories

Each person's life is full of a rich set of events in work, life and relationships. Some events will be of success, positive emotions, overcoming challenges and making positive changes. Some events will be less helpful to remember.

- What memories do you need to recall to fully experience the state?
- What memories do you need to let go in order to fully experience the state?

Thinking Patterns

Whatever a person is paying attention to will contain some elements in the foreground and some in the background. How are you thinking in each moment, and what strategies are you using to respond to the current situation, directly influence your state.

- What are you thinking just before you experience the state?
- What do you think about that keeps you experiencing the state?
- What is important to you when you experience the state?

Future Expectations

Whenever you make a representation of the future you set up a filter for experience that makes it more likely that what you expect to happen will happen. Your belief of what could happen makes it possible to happen.

- What do you have that help you experience the state?
- What expectations do you need to let go of to experience the state?

BUILDING A RESOURCEFUL STATE

There are two main ways we can think about an experience, associated or disassociated. Association refers to being fully in an experience; seeing, hearing and feeling what you saw, heard or felt. Dissociation is viewing oneself being in the situation or feeling separated from all or a part of your body.

- Dissociation is useful for designing desired states
- Association is useful for accessing desired states

The Resource Triangle

The resource triangle uses association and dissociation to enable a person to design resourceful states to collapse an unhelpful present state. If the resourceful state is stronger than the present state, then the resulting new state will be a resourceful place from which your client can generate new solutions for the future.

1. *Define the present situation you'd like to change*
   Identify a situation where your client feels they are in a stuck, un-resourceful or problem state that they would like to change.

2. *Identify three separate locations*
   Select three distinct spaces. Identify them as PS (Present State), D (Disassociated), and R (Resourceful State).

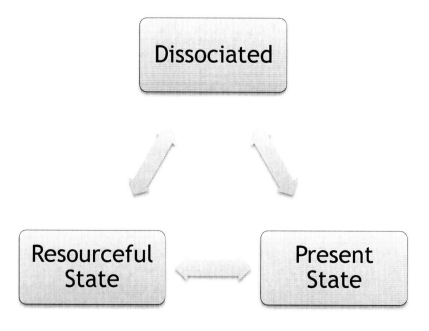

3. **Briefly step into the Present State space**
   Associate into the unwanted state for a brief moment to connect with the
   unwanted state that you want to move away from.

4. **Step into the Disassociated Space**
   Disassociate from the problem state, leaving all those feelings over there (point to
   the "PS" space).
   Turn and look toward the Resourceful State space. Identify several resourceful
   states that would be appropriate to the current situation. For example, choose
   humour, confidence, curiosity, etc. See the resources over there (point to the
   space). See the "you" holding those resources. For each resourceful state describe
   how you look and sound if you were full in that state. Make sure the sum of the
   resourceful states is more powerful than the present state.

   Look over at the resource space "R". Know that in a minute you are going to step
   into that space and fully associate into that resource.

5. **Step into the Resourceful State space**
   Wrap the resourceful state(s) fully around you. For each resourceful state identify
   a specific time when you were experiencing it and see what you were seeing at
   the time, hear what you were hearing at the time and feel all the feelings. Feel
   this state in your entire body.

   When you have completely associated into all the resourceful states...

6. **Step into the Present State space again**
   Moving only as fast as you can take all these positive and resourceful feelings with
   you, step into the present state. Take a moment and let this fully integrate.

7. **Step outside the triangle**
   Take a deep breath and notice how the situation is different now.
   What new solutions are now available to you that were not available before?
   What options and choices do you now have available to you?

8. **Revisit the three positions again as required**

9. **What is the next smallest step to take?**

ACCESSING RESOURCEFUL STATES

The events and memories of our life provide a rich resource of useful states, for example the first time we rode a bike, asked someone out, were offered a job or passed a test. As we go through life we often forget to remember that within those experiences is the knowledge of how to learn through trial and error, be confident to speak out, be believed in and apply our skills.

> "This time, like all times, is a very good one, if we but know what to do with it."
>
> Ralph Waldo Emerson

The NLP presupposition *'we already have all the resources we need'* reminds us that whenever we experience problems and challenges, the ability to meet and overcome these challenges is within us. As a coach, working with a person's timeline is a very effective way of helping someone access past resourceful states to use in the present and future. The basic process involves 5 steps:

EVENT   NOW

1. Float up from now so you can look at yourself in the now and your timeline laid out in front of you.
2. Go back to a specific time and look at the memory of an event concerning the younger you.
3. See the younger you feeling the particular resourceful state. Associate to the memory to feel the good feelings even stronger.
4. Disassociate and gather the learnings by asking your unconscious mind what there is to learn that is positive and beneficial you now.
5. Return to the now and integrate yourself fully and completely.

The process works excellently when it is physically walked or when completed as a visualisation. Choose an approach that suits the context for your coaching and your clients preferences – if they are good at making pictures use a visualisation, if they like to be moving then use an area outside to walk their timeline.

Example of a Timeline Visualisation to Collect Learning

1. **Set up the timeline**
   - *"All our memories have a particular date stamp to them, a time when they occurred. We all store our memories somewhere, and one way to do that is to imagine them stretched out on a line with your past memories in one direction and your future memories in another"*
   - *"Now, if I were to ask your conscious mind where your past is and where your future is I have an idea you might say it's from right to left or from front to back or up to down or in some direction from you in relationship to your body but it's not your conscious concept I'm interested in, it's your unconscious"*
   - *"So, if I were to ask your unconscious mind where is your past, to what direction would you point? And if I were to ask in what direction is the future, where would you point? And can you imagine those two locations being linked by a line?"*
   - *"Now, in whatever way is right for you, float up above your timeline so you are looking down on now"*

2. **Go back to a resourceful memory**
   - *"There are times in life when you have achieved some great things, perhaps passing a test or getting a particular job or making a special commitment or achieving a really great goal. Bring to mind one of those times now that is particularly relevant for the challenge you are now facing"*
   - *"Float back in time so that you are looking down on the particular event. What's happening in the memory? What were you doing, what were you thinking, what were you feeling?"*

3. **Re-experience the memory**
   - *"If you would like, go back into the memory and enjoy the positive aspects of the experience fully"*
   - *"Float out of the memory again so you are looking down on it"*

4. **Collect the learnings**
   - *"As you look down at that event now, what can you notice about how you achieved your goal or challenge that could be a helpful resource for you to use in your life now? What have you learned that is useful to you now? And what else... And what else..."*
   - *"Store those learnings in the place you store such learnings"*

5. **Return to the present**
   - *"Return to now on your timeline bringing all your resources with you"*
   - *"Come back into the room and open your eyes when you feel integrated"*

ANCHORING A CHOSEN STATE

Being able to access a certain emotional state when you choose is a very useful resource to help avoid an unhelpful feeling or access a powerful or motivating feeling. Setting an anchor brings your emotional state within your influence – a relaxation anchor can help relieve stress; an energetic anchor can help a trainer be ready to

> *"Anchoring is a tendency for any one element of an experience to bring back the entire experience"*
>
> *Bandler & Grinder*
> *(Frogs into Princes)*

work with a group; a confidence anchor can help a competitor be ready to perform at their best; a curiosity anchor can help a manager adopt a coaching role.

Anchors are automatically set as part of everyday life, a certain look, object or song will immediately bring an experience or feeling. An anchor consists of a specific trigger linked to a specific emotional state. Some triggers are external and particular to the context in which you want the anchor to fire - something the person hears, sees or touches. Some triggers can be internal, like imagining a particular image or making a specific touch.

4 Keys to Anchoring

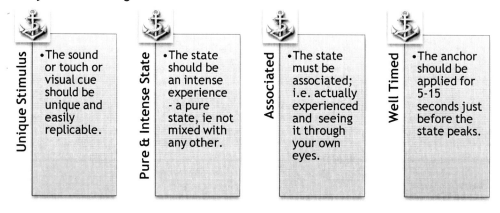

Unique Stimulus
- The sound or touch or visual cue should be unique and easily replicable.

Pure & Intense State
- The state should be an intense experience - a pure state, ie not mixed with any other.

Associated
- The state must be associated; i.e. actually experienced and seeing it through your own eyes.

Well Timed
- The anchor should be applied for 5-15 seconds just before the state peaks.

Using Anchoring in Coaching

As a coach it can be useful to anchor a particular state with your client or group, either overtly or covertly, to assist them at times in the coaching process. You may also help someone set an anchor for themselves so that they can re-access a resourceful state when they choose.

- What would be a useful anchor for you as a coach?
- What anchors would be useful for a coaching session?
- What might be resourceful anchors for your clients?

The Self Anchoring Process

1. *Decide on the anchor you want and choose the unique trigger. Knuckles work well or a pinch between thumb and little finger, or seeing a particular object. Make sure the trigger is not an everyday occurrence.*

2. *Get yourself into the emotional state you want to anchor intensely and fully associated. Use all the senses (sight, sound, feel, touch and taste) to remember a time when you were in the desired state. See what you saw, hear what you heard, feel what you felt. Even better, if you want to anchor the state of peak performance, be in that state!*

3. *Notice when you start to go into the state. As you near the peak set the anchor for 5-15 seconds by applying a firm pressure using as little an area as possible or focussing on the chosen object. Release just as the state comes to a peak.*

4. *Repeat steps 2 and 3 several times.*

5. *Test. Distract yourself by doing something in a different state to the one anchored. When you are not expecting it fire the anchor and notice what happens. If you bring back the state, the anchor is set. If not, go back to step 2 and repeat.*

6. *Firing the anchor and allowing yourself to fully feel the associated emotional state will strengthen the anchor.*

Creating a Circle of Excellence

1. *Imagine a circle on the ground in front of you*

2. *Identify the first resource you would like to place in the circle*

3. *Step into the circle and associate to the state fully, feeling it in your fingers and toes and throughout your body. As the state peaks, step out of the circle.*

4. *Identify the second resource you would like to place in the circle*

5. *Step into the circle and associate to the state fully, feeling it in your fingers and toes and throughout your body. As the state peaks, step out of the circle.*

6. *Repeat adding as many resources as you need to your circle*

7. *Imagine picking up your circle and carrying it with you so that it will always be available when you need it*

8. *When you need it, imaging placing your circle on the ground and step into it to activate the resourceful states. Feel the feelings fully and perform excellently.*

SUCCESS IS AN ALTERED STATE

Each day is a kaleidoscope of different experiences, each allowing a different state of consciousness to the foreground and other states to the background. We go in and out of altered states all day in order to perform at our best.

> "Trance is at the very foundation of human experience"
>
> Richard Bandler

In his Guide to Trance-Formation Richard Bandler writes *"There are as many types of altered states as there are people to imagine them. The possibilities are limitless... the biggest misconception is that hypnotic states are rare and under somebody else's control. The truth is you actually have more control over yourself in an altered state than you do in the waking state."*

A useful altered state is that of trance, one which Milton Erickson described as *"a state in which the client pays attention to what is really, immediately important, and disregards information that isn't immediately important."* In an uptime trance, a person is paying attention to information that is outside them - a great state for coaching, training and presenting. In a downtime trance a person is paying attention to internal sensations and thoughts.

> "Trance is really fast paced. You are constantly dancing and jumping around."
>
> Lewis Carroll
> (Alice in Wonderland)

Altered States in Coaching

Great athletes and performers go into altered states to perform naturally and be 'in the zone' or 'in flow'. You have to go into a slightly altered state just to be able to spell a word or recall a particular experience.

In a mild altered state of trance your client or audience will still be aware of their surroundings but may have more of their focus on something else like their breathing, relaxing their muscles, a daydream, or listening to a good story being told.

When coaching you can create a pleasant, relaxing altered state to allow your client to:

- Fully re-experience memories that are resourceful
- Follow a relaxation routine to wind down, aid sleeping or de-stress
- Visualise new behaviours in future contexts

Creating an Altered State

In addition to the three basic ways of eliciting a state (change physiology and breathing, remembering a time in detail and be in the state yourself) the language you use and your voice tone, tempo and volume are powerful tools. To create an altered state, use sentences that are artfully vague and direct attention to what is helpful and allow the listener to complete the specific details themselves. The Milton Model language patterns are ideal for this – *"As you relax a little more... and you are aware of your breathing changing... you might find an unexpected pleasant feeling comes to mind... now... that offers you certain pleasant sensations... that can spread through your body... and easily last..."*

To induce a calm, relaxed state
- Speak slowly and quietly
- Use your deepest voice
- Relax yourself completely
- Use deep, slow breathing
- Leave gaps

To induce an alert, vibrant state
- Speak quickly and loudly
- Use a variety of tones
- Use shallow, quick breathing
- Ask questions
- Be high energy

Re-experiencing a pleasant memory

This is one example of how you could help someone use the altered state of trance to access a resourceful state.

1. *Close your eyes and then spend a couple of minutes getting really comfortable*

2. *Become aware of your breathing, notice the location and depth of each breath*

3. *Adopt a passive attitude – whatever happens will be OK, your unconscious mind will keep you safe*

4. *As you focus on your breathing rhythm allow a pleasant and resourceful memory to come to mind*

5. *Go back into that memory and really see what you saw at the time, hear what you heard and feel all the pleasant and resourceful feelings that you felt...*

6. *Ask yourself "how can I use the learning from this experience to assist me in a current challenge now"*

7. *Come back into the room and open your eyes only as soon as you are feeling alert and refreshed*

THE RELAXATION RESPONSE

In a busy world with the seemingly constant need for speed, decisiveness and action many people can find they are spending many minutes each day in a state of high arousal or even stress. This fight or flight response is an automatic reaction of the sympathetic nervous system to exciting or stressful situations. It is designed to prepare your body for action or emergency. It shunts your blood to your muscles and increases your blood pressure, heart rate and breathing rate, enabling you to cope with stressful situations. The stress response leads to narrow thinking and experiencing it too frequently leads to high blood pressure.

Dr. Herbert Benson has described a physiological response that is the opposite of the fight-or flight (stress) response. The relaxation response provides balance and activates your parasympathetic nervous system to ensure you actively digest food, promote recovery and maintain your blood pressure, heart rate and breathing rate at a low level. Dr. Benson's research conducted at the Harvard Medical School documented that **relaxation response** based approaches used in combination with nutrition, exercise, and stress management interventions **resulted in the alleviation of many stress-related medical disorders.**

- Teaching someone the relaxation response can help them manage stress and anxiety
- Creating the relaxation response elicits an altered state when a person is more open to suggestions

The altered state of the Relaxation Response can help the conscious and unconscious minds to communicate easily. It can also create what the Native American elder Stalking Wolf calls a state of Sacred Silence where you are able to connect to your inner vision or spirit.

Creating the relaxation response requires four basic steps which can be adapted to suit many different activities:

Quiet Environment
- Choose a quiet, calm environment with as few distractions as possible.

Comfortable Position
- Be in a relaxed state of comfort in whatever you are doing.

Concentration Point
- Focus and concentrate your mind on something, such as **counting as you breathe,** enjoying a memory, **listening to a story,** focusing intensely, etc.

Passive Attitude
- Allow any thoughts that come into your mind to freely go out of your mind, adopt a let it happen attitude.

Dr. Benson describes a tried and scientifically validated method of creating the Relaxation Response as follows:

Self Relaxation

1. *Sit quietly in a comfortable position*

2. *Close your eyes*

3. *Deeply relax all you muscles. Begin at your feet and progress up to the top of your head.*

4. *Become aware of your breathing. Breathe in through your nose. As you breathe out count silently to yourself "ONE". Continue focussing on breathing out; Breathe IN . . . OUT . . . . ."TWO"; IN . . . OUT . . . . ."THREE"; etc. Breathe easily and naturally.*

5. *Continue for 10 to 20 minutes. You can open your eyes to check the time, but do not use an alarm as it can set up an unhelpful state of anticipation.*

6. *When you finish, sit quietly for several minutes. At first keep your eyes closed and when you are ready open your eyes. Do not stand up for a few minutes.*

7. *Do not worry about whether you are successful at achieving a deep level of relaxation. Maintain a passive attitude and allow relaxation to occur at its own pace. When distracting thoughts occur, notice them with an attitude of curiosity and return to your breathing.*

8. *With practice the relaxation response will come easily. Practice the technique once or twice daily. Do not practice within 2 hours after any meal since the digestive processes seem to interfere with the elicitation of the Relaxation Response.*

Adapted from "The Relaxation Response" by
Herbert Benson M.D. (1975) Pages 162-163

PROGRESSIVE RELAXATION ROUTINE

Progressive relaxation is an effective way of reducing physical anxiety. In the Mental Game Plan by Stephen Bull, Chris Shambrook and John Albinson they describe deep relaxation as a very useful way of recovering from a hard days work or training session as well as generally reducing the physical effects of stress.

Relaxation is a very individual experience and people vary enormously in what works for them. The more you practice the easier it becomes and you can discover a sequence and routine that works for you. To enable you to enjoy the experience as fully as possible avoid using an alarm as it can set up a state of expecting the alarm to go off. You can open your eyes to check the time if you need to. The more you trust yourself and practice the routine, the more natural, enjoyable and beneficial it can be.

1. *Choose a calm environment. Perhaps put on some relaxing music.*

2. *Set a time for your relaxation session. Decide on how long you are going to take for the session and say to yourself: "Unconscious mind please assist me for the next ___ minutes in enjoying a pleasant and relaxing experience by keeping me safe and waking me if needed"*

3. *Close your eyes and then spend a couple of minutes to **get really comfortable** and tune-in to your body. How does your body feel right now - which areas are the warmest, which coldest, which have been most tense, which areas are you not aware of and which areas are the most relaxed?*

4. *Become aware of your breathing. Breathe easily and naturally through your nose. Notice the location and depth of each breath.*

5. *Adopt a passive attitude - whatever happens will be OK, your unconscious mind will assist you to achieve the right depth of relaxation for you. Allow relaxation to occur at its own pace. When distracting thoughts occur, notice them with an attitude of curiosity and return to your breathing.*

6. *Focus on your breathing rhythm. Take 10 deep breaths to establish a slow, steady breathing rhythm. Each time you breathe out, feel more relaxed and feel some tension begin to disappear. Focus on breathing out and silently count to yourself as you complete each out breath one, two, three, etc."*

7. *When you feel ready, focus on your right arm. Clench your fist tightly, count to 10, and then slowly open out your fingers and relax your hand and arm completely. Feel your arm go heavy and sink into the floor or chair. Repeat this process once. **Then run through the process for your left arm.***

8. **Focus on your right leg**. *Tighten the muscles in your leg, count to 10, and then relax all the muscles completely. Feel your leg go heavy and let it comfortably sink downwards. Repeat this process once.* **Then run through the same process for your left leg.**

9. **Turn your attention to your neck and shoulders**. *Relax all the muscles completely. Count to ten and with each breath let the muscles in your neck and the back of your shoulders relax even more.*

10. **Focus on your face**. *Relax all the muscles in this area. In particular focus on smoothing out the muscles in your forehead. Relax your cheeks, your eyes and your jaw.*

11. **Focus on relaxing your whole body**. *Concentrate on a relaxed feeling in your fingertips, toes and forehead.*

12. **Spend several minutes enjoying this relaxed feeling**. *Continue listening to your music or imagining yourself in a place where you can feel completely relaxed and at ease. This may be on the beach, by a swimming pool, on a boat, in a forest, up a mountain, etc. Go to that place in your mind and really enjoy the pleasant relaxed feelings of being there, seeing what you see and hearing what you hear.*

13. **When you are ready, return from this place**. *Countdown silently, and slowly, from 10 to 1. As you do so, bend and stretch your arms, move your head from side to side and gradually bring yourself back. As you get to number one, you can open your eyes and tell yourself that you feel relaxed, rested and refreshed.*

6

Shifting

Perspectives

"The greatest personal limitation is to be found not in the things you want to do and can't, but in the things you've never considered doing."

Richard Bandler

FRAMING QUESTIONS

All questions lead the answerer by asking them to include certain elements of information and exclude others. A question sets a direction and provides a frame for the answer to fit in. Useful questions are often those that are outside the listener's current frame of reference.

- Do you ask questions that direct the client to more resourceful outcomes, emotional states, thinking processes, behaviours or learnings?

Outcome Frame

The outcome frame directs and focuses attention towards the goals, outcomes, resources, solutions or strengths you have or can get.

- What do you want?
- What options do you have?
- What resources can you use?
- What is a possible solution?
- What can you learn from this?
- What needs to happen next?

Problem Frame

How does someone maintain and experience their problem. Sometimes unless a client is actually feeling what it's like to have their problem they cannot easily connect with the motivation to change.

- Who owns the problem?
- What exactly is the problem?
- How is that a problem for you?
- What is standing in the way of a solution?

Backtrack Frame

Use the backtrack frame to review or summarise using your clients key words and tonalities. Backtrack to make sure you understand the other person / group and to recap on information relevant to their outcome.

Discovery Frame

A discovery frame is at the heart of the NLP attitudes of curiosity and possibility. By modelling the current situation you can uncover the unconscious patterns of thinking and behaviour that create either limitations or successes for your client.

- How exactly do you do that?
- What thoughts lead to that feeling?
- What behaviour follows that feeling?

Worst Case Frame

When confronted with change, some people look first, and often exclusively, at the risks and potential downsides, while simultaneously under-rating potential benefits. Applying the worst case frame can help someone avoid focussing on unhelpful generalisations of the potential effects of a change.

- What is the worst that can happen?

Best Case Frame

Considering the best-case scenario can orientate someone in an optimistic, hopeful, goal-oriented, and empowered way.

- Given how things are right now, what is the best outcome for you?

Contrast Frame

Gregory Bateson described information as *"the difference that makes the difference"*. Using the contrast frame you can evaluate information. The contrast frame is especially good for comparing average with excellence, problem to no-problem, low-confidence in one context with confidence in another context, etc.

- How is this different to _____?
- What are the important variations?
- What is it that makes this stand out?
- What is different between _____ and _____?

Relevancy Frame

You can help your client evaluate the usefulness of the information they share by considering the frame of relevancy.

- How is this relevant?
- How is this not relevant?

Agreement Frame

When negotiating or running a meeting, setting an agreement frame will enable all parties to keep focussed on contributing towards the desired outcome.

- What is it that we can agree on?

As-If Frame

The as-if frame engages a creative approach to discovering resources and solutions. It is a generative approach that encourages the listener to generate new ideas without reference to possibly inappropriate prior assumptions of inability, limits and constraints. For example *"The question isn't why do you drink? The real question is what would you do if you didn't?"*

- If you had already achieved your goal, how would you be different?
- What happens if you act as if you have the resources available now?
- If you knew, what is the solution you have not been aware of until now?
- If you were wise and knowledgeable, what advice would you give yourself?
- Imagine the problem has been solved, what would you see, hear, feel or do?

Ecology Frame

Using the ecology frame assists your client in exploring the consequences within the wider systems of family, friends, work interests and their world.

- What would you gain?
- What could you lose?
- How might this change affect those around you and the wider world?

REFRAMING TO CHANGE MEANINGS

A frame is a way of looking at a memory, situation or event that shapes the meaning we give it. Reframing is the art of giving the person or group another perspective from which to view their current situation. It is a way of inviting someone to expand their map of the world.

Reframing Limitations

When a person expresses a limitation it is usually a statement of belief. Typically people take beliefs and treat them as if they were facts – something that is fixed or stationary, something that you can't get around. In practice of course facts can change - the world is no longer flat. If the person is open to change being appropriate and desirable a reframe will open up the possibility for change.

Establishing a full Belief Statement

Some of the best results in reframing come when you have taken the time to establish a full belief statement from your group or client that describes their perceived limitation or unhelpful meaning. When the person has been holding on to a belief for a long time and has generalised it to be at identity level, like *"I'm no good with numbers"* or *"I'm just not a confident person"*, getting a full statement will connect them back to their original experience. For example:

What stops you getting what you want?	*"I can't do it"*
What specifically can't you do?	*"I can't trust myself"*
What makes it that way?	*"I messed up the first time so I can't trust myself now"*

Creating Reframes

Content and context reframes are the foundation for many different types of reframe (Robert Dilts identifies at least 14 different patterns in his book Sleight of Mouth). Just because you use a reframe, it doesn't guarantee the other person will change immediately.

When using reframing, usually the more different perspectives you can offer a person the better. It is hard to know exactly which one will work best for the particular person or group in advance so just use a spirit of playfulness to try several out. Get the ball rolling consciously then allow your unconscious to come up with them spontaneously – often the reframe you least expect will work the best, works the best.

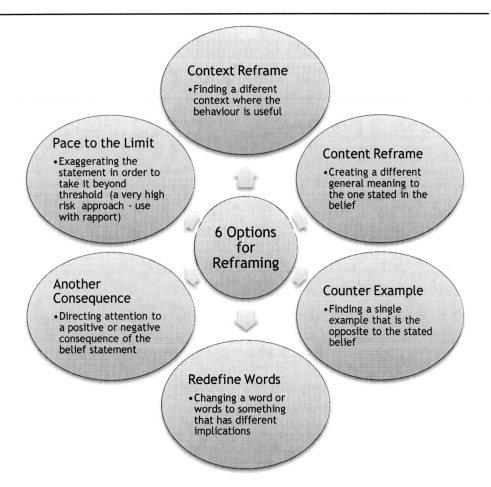

Context Reframe
- Finding a diferent context where the behaviour is useful

Pace to the Limit
- Exaggerating the statement in order to take it beyond threshold (a very high risk approach - use with rapport)

Content Reframe
- Creating a different general meaning to the one stated in the belief

6 Options for Reframing

Another Consequence
- Directing attention to a positive or negative consequence of the belief statement

Counter Example
- Finding a single example that is the opposite to the stated belief

Redefine Words
- Changing a word or words to something that has different implications

For example: **"I won't be a good Coach because I'm scared"**

- "At least you can be a good actor in a horror film about a coach"
- "That just means you care about doing a good job as a coach"
- "Has there ever been a time when you were scared and yet you were able to do something good"
- "You'll be fine as a coach because you are apprehensive"
- "If you won't be a good coach because you are scared then that just means the more you coach the more you have the opportunity to be a great coach"
- "You are right, you'll probably be a 100% unhelpful coach and the person will end up much worse because you are so frightened you can't look up or speak a single word"

REVERSAL QUESTIONS

The problem contains the solution

Sometimes your client is so stuck in their problem or situation that they can't see the wood for the trees. They may be trapped in a pattern of thinking and talking about what they don't want and find it hard to start talking about what they do want. Asking 'reversal questions' can help you model the structure of your clients experience and change the way they re-present their problem.

> "In the reversal method one takes things as they are and then turns them round, inside out, upside down, back to front. Then one sees what happens."
>
> Edward de Bono
> (Lateral Thinking)

Reversal questions create movement, and where there is movement there can be change.

1. *Tell me about your current situation.*

2. *What exactly is the problem you have been experiencing?*

    • *When did the problem first start?*

    • *How often does it occur?*

    • *How long does it last?*

    • *Who is affected by the problem?*

3. *Where have you been noticing the problem (in what context)?*

4. *What do you need to keep on doing, in order to maintain this problem?*

5. *What beliefs do you have to hold for this problem to persist?*

6. *What everything has to be there for this problem to occur?*

7. *What would you need to do to make this problem worse?*

8. *How do you know when you are about to have this problem?*

9. *How can you teach someone else to have to this problem?*

    • *Teach me now... what must I do, think, believe and value?*

    • *What kind of person do I have to be to have this problem as well?*

10. *In order to create this problem in a different context what would you need to do?*

11. *What do you do differently in those contexts where you don't have the problem?*

12. *There are some people who don't have this problem. What are they doing that is different from what you do?*

- *What do they never do that you sometimes (or often) do?*

- *What advice could you give them from your own personal experience that would help them to create this problem?*

13. *What is the quickest and best way that you can solve this problem and really enjoy the process and learn a whole lot else at the same time as well?*

14. *How can you use this learning in other ways and other places?*

Reverse your self-talk – ask yourself a solution question

Often when we do certain things and we don't get the results we want we will ask ourselves a really lousy question like *"why did I do that?"* or *"I'm useless, why does this always happen?"* Of course your unconscious mind will then willingly supply a whole host of reasons why that happened and strengthen the neural pathways to make it even more likely it will happen again in the future. Anyone who plays tennis and has just hit a bad shot and used one of these questions knows the results of this problem thinking.

A great alternative is to ask a better question in order to activate different neural pathways and set a direction of thought that includes new possibilities and solutions. You could ask questions like:

- "What can I learn from this?"
- "How can I do things differently next time?"
- "How can this experience be useful to me in the future?"

SHIFTING PERCEPTUAL POSITIONS

It has been said that one of the best ways to understand another person's point of view is to walk a mile in his or her shoes. Using perceptual positions you mentally review (or preview) a situation from a number of different standpoints in order to enrich your appreciation of what is involved.

> *"Wisdom comes from multiple perspectives"*
>
> *Gregory Bateson*

The idea of multiple perceptual positions in NLP was inspired by Gregory Bateson who proposed that double (or triple) descriptions are better than one. Virginia Satir would also sometimes guide a family member to stand in everyone elses' actual shoes, until they understood better other's position and feelings. By adopting different perceptual positions you can develop new choices for responding to events.

> *"Do not evaluate until you have, through multiple descriptions, gained news of difference."*
>
> *John Grinder and Judith DeLozier*
> *(Turtles All The Way Down)*

For example: A day when it starts to snow heavily and doesn't stop looks very different from the viewpoint of a pupil, parent, teacher and the school bus company. Knowing what to do is almost inevitably harder to solve if the Head teacher only appreciates their own viewpoint and not those of others involved and the system as a whole.

 YOU

Knowing your own reality, your thoughts, feelings, beliefs, values, goals and needs.

1st position is essential for a strong sense of knowing yourelf and your boundaries as a coach.

 OTHER

The other's point of view - how they think, act and what they value, believe and feel.

2nd position is helpful as a coach in order to show empathy and compassion.

 META

A detached perspective able to look at the system as a whole that contains you and the other.

3rd position is helpful for looking at the wider concequences for coach and client and others.

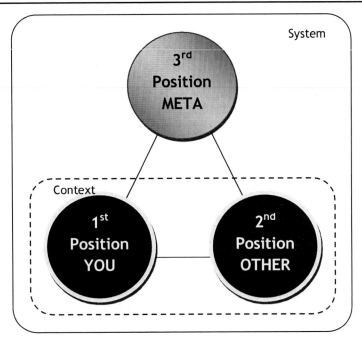

1. *Identify a relationship to explore*

2. *1st Position - YOU*
   See the situation through your own eyes. Be aware of your own thoughts and feelings and how they are impacting on the relationship. What are your own needs? What do you want to have happen?

3. *2nd Position - OTHER*
   Imagine what it is like to be the significant other in the situation. Put yourself in their shoes - as if you are looking back at yourself, seeing, hearing, and feeling as the other person would given their own map of the world. What are their needs? What do they want to have happen?

4. *3rd Position - META*
   Take a detached viewpoint and look at the system as a whole. Imagine looking at yourself and the other person 'over there' seeing the two of them interacting. Pay particular attention to actual behaviour, body language and the sound of their voices. What helpful wisdom or advice would you (or someone else) give the you 'over there'?

5. *Bring what you have learned back to the you in the 1st position.*
   What is different, what has changed? Do you need to revisit any of the positions again?

SHIFTING SUB-MODALITIES

Sub-modalities are the finer distinctions we make within a particular representational system. For instance if you create a picture in your mind of your front door at home, then brightness, focus and motion are some of the finer distinctions of the image.

Each particular thought or memory, when we bring it mind will have two elements - the content and the sub-modalities. Sub-Modalities are how we code our experiences. We create different meanings by using different sub-modalities to code our experience, for example someone we like and someone we dislike or what you believe and what you do not believe. Changing sub-modalities changes a person's thinking processes.

Exploring Sub-modalities

Often the client will describe the sub-modalities of their experience with the words they use, for instance *"I feel a **weight on my shoulders**"* or *"I'm just not **clear** what to do next"*. As coach, you can help the client explore different options by taking the sub-modality literally, for example: *"how big is the weight?"*, *"whose weight is it?"*, *"how could you lighten the load?"* or *"how can you sharpen your focus?"*

Some of the sub-modality distinctions to explore in an internal representation are:

Visual

The qualities of the internal image a person is aware of:

Colour / Black and White

Brightness (or dullness)

Contrast (vivid or washed out)

Focus / Blurred

Size of Picture (get dimensions)

Border (yes/no, panoramic)

Associated / Disassociated

Distance (get dimensions)

Moving / Still (speed, direction)

Auditory

The qualities of the internal sounds a person is aware of:

Location (source)

Pitch (high-low)

Tonality (hard-soft-grating)

Volume (how loud)

Tempo (fast-slow)

Duration (continuous-intermittent)

Kinaesthetic

The qualities of the internal feelings a person is aware of:

Quality (describe the body sensation)

Intensity (strength of sensation)

Location (in your body)

Shape (describe it)

Movement (continuous/waves/none)

Direction (where does it start)

Critical Sub-Modalities

Amongst the many possible sub-modalities for a person, there will often be several 'critical sub-modalities'. They differ between people and contexts, and can be identified by observation as you vary the sub-modalities one by one. A change within these critical sub-modalities will often correlate with a near-immediate subjective change in the feelings or sensations that accompany the internal representation.

> *"for any given experience there is a difference that makes the difference - a sub-modality adjustment that results in a different response"*
>
> *Richard Bandler &
> Will MacDonald*

- Knowing their critical sub-modalities can help a person take control of their internal experience

Shifting Sub-modalities

Since the combination of sub-modalities defines how a person relates to a particular thought or memory, if you adjust the sub-modalities you can change the associated meaning. This can be very useful in helping people transform stuck thinking and /or their feelings towards something.

1. *Ensure the person is in the state associated with the particular thought or memory*

2. *Have the person pay attention to the internal image they see*

3. *Shift the sub-modalities of the picture to their complimentary opposite so that the person is relating to the particular thought or memory in a more resourceful way*
   - 5 distinctions that are often a good starting point are location, size, focus, distance and brightness.

4. *Adjust other sub-modalities (auditory and kinaesthetic) as needed*

5. *What is the next step to take?*

Map-across Sub-Modalities

This key NLP technique is based on shifting the sub-modalities of one internal representation to match the sub-modalities of another. This process can create very fast and lasting change.

- Map across the sub-modalities of dislike something to like something.
- Map across the sub-modalities of limiting belief to a neutral belief or want to believe to definitely believe.

SHIFTING ATTENTION

Foreground and Background Switch

Whenever we place our attention somewhere, there are elements of our experience that will be in the foreground and some in the background. The foreground contains what is central, important, focal, meaningful to the present moment. The background contains what is irrelevant, unimportant, immaterial to the present moment. The meaning and impact that a particular experience holds for us depends upon what aspects of it we regard as the foreground and what we perceive to be the background. When we shift attention between foreground to

> *"For me, a landscape does not exist in its own right, since its appearance changes at every moment; but the surrounding atmosphere brings it to life - the light and the air which vary continually. For me, it is only the surrounding atmosphere which gives subjects their true value."*
>
> Claude Monet

background it is possible to reveal some new information that may prove valuable.

- What aspects of the current situation are in the foreground?
- What aspects of the current situation are in the background?
- What can you notice that you haven't noticed before?

Time for a Change

When we are born and for the first months of our life we only really know the present moment. All our responses are based on what is happening and all our requests are based on our current needs. There is only one time, and it is now. As we grow up and our bank of experience grows, we begin to construct a way of separating our memories. In the western world we often create the distinctions of past, present and future in order to code our experiences.

From these 3 distinctions, we typically develop a preference for which one we most often use to understand, solve problems and learn from experience. This will often be illustrated in the language a person uses, especially when they are focussing on a problem or challenge. For example:

Past What has happened	Present What is happening	Future What could happen
•The problem is... •What's worked before is...	•I'm feeling... •What I want is...	•A solution is... •What will go wrong is...

Within all experiences, past, present and future, there are some elements that will be helpful and some that will be unhelpful. **In general it is usually helpful for a person's past to be regarded as a source of information and positive resources** for the present. Living based on unhelpful emotions, events or decisions in the past can limit a person's experience in the present. Although we can't control or precisely predict the future, it is usually beneficial to consider the present as shaping the future. How we are feeling, thinking, acting at any moment will have a significant impact on the experiences we have in the next moment and in the future. Some examples:

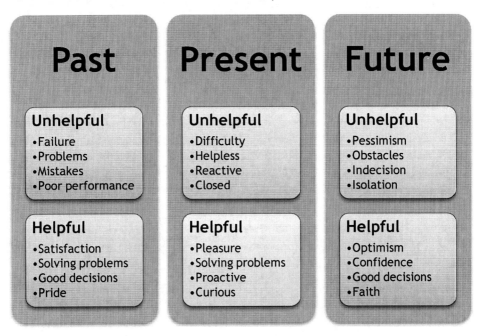

In coaching you might hear your client describe their situation and cause and place a particular emphasis on one time period. Helping your client shift their attention to a different time period can assist them to identify resources that have been hidden until now.

- How has the way you have been thinking about the past/present/future affected your situation?
- What would happen if you focussed on the past/present/future?
- How can your past/present/future be a resource for you?

LEARNING FROM THE FUTURE

When we are in the present and looking at the future there are always many paths and options, each one leading in a different direction. How do we know the right one to take?

In reality the answer is very simple - take a step and evaluate. In practice many clients often get caught up evaluating before they have taken a step. When this happens they can spend their time guessing what might happen and then deciding what is or isn't the easiest / fastest / cheapest option. They put so much effort into choosing the "best option" they never even get around to starting.

This process usually happens because a person is either not in touch with what they want or doesn't have the confidence that the first step will lead them to their desired outcome.

- Setting a well formed outcome helps clients know where they are going
- There is always a straight line looking back from where you are now to where you have been
- Stepping into the future and looking back towards now helps clients gain confidence that the steps they plan to take will lead to the outcomes they want

Walking out along a timeline is a great way to get a future perspective on a challenge or action. Invite your client to use a pattern in the carpet or the space between some trees in the local park to represent their past, present and future.

1. *Identify a clear state, behaviour or outcome to take into a specific future context*
2. *Ask the person to imagine their timeline on the floor in front of them. Locate now on the timeline, and the direction of the past and the future.*

3. *Walk along the timeline and look down on a future event*

- *"Now, walk alongside the timeline to a particular event in the future so that you are looking down on the event."*

NOW   FUTURE

4. **Associate to the positive experience**

   - *"Step into the event and enjoy the feelings of successfully behaving in the way you want to behave and achieving your outcome."*
   - *"What are you seeing, what are you hearing, what are you doing, how are you feeling?"*

5. **Step out of the event and collect the learnings**

   - *"Step off the timeline and look down on you going through that event. Ask your unconscious what there is to learn from the event, the learning of which is positive and useful to you?"* (PAUSE)
   - *"Anything else? Anything else?"* (CHECK YOU HAVE ALL THE LEARNINGS)
   - *"Store the learnings in the place you store such learnings"* (and record them for your client)

6. **Look back towards now and learn**

   - *"Looking back towards now notice any significant steps that you took that made it possible for you to behave in the way you want and achieve your outcome. How did you overcome any obstacles? What key resources helped you along the way?"*
   - *"Store the learnings in the place you store such learnings"* (and record them for your client)

7. **Come back to above now**

   - *"Walk back to now looking down on your timeline collecting any gems on the way. Ready, go!"*

8. **What is your next step that will take you in a useful direction?**

   - *"As you look towards the future, what resources do you now have that will help you"*
   - *"Notice any key moments on the way to achieving your outcome, and how you successfully met any challenges"*
   - *"What is the next smallest step that will take you towards your outcome?"*

RESOLVING INTERNAL CONFLICTS

A fairly common coaching situation is where your client is describing being torn between two options, *"on the one hand I want more responsibility at work and on the other hand I want more time with my family."* The pull between the two parts is so strong that they either create an uncomfortable feeling of cognitive dissonance or physical distress or unease. The NLP Parts Integration Process (visual squash) is an elegant way of resolving this internal conflict.

> *"Each part has a valid function and a valid way of accomplishing its function, but they step on each others toes. It's not that one part is "making you do it"; it's that two parts are each doing something useful, but the ways they are doing it conflict with each other"*
>
> *Bandler and Grinder*
> (Reframing)

Often your client will helpfully describe the conflict as they discuss the situation and cause with you or you may notice them making gestures to one location for one part and to another location for the other part. As you check out this incongruence your client will either confirm that the gestures represent two parts in conflict or suggest that they have a different meaning altogether. Where the desired outcome is to resolve the inner conflict, the process for integrating two parts is:

1. **Determine the parts in conflict**
   - Determine one of the parts involved.
   - Identify the other part that is in greatest conflict with this part

2. **Place one part in one hand and make it 'real'.**
   - Create a visual, auditory and kinaesthetic representation for the part in that hand. An alternative here is to select an object that represents the part concerned. When coaching outdoors the natural world is full of potential objects – stones, sticks etc.
   - Ask this part what resources and strengths it brings – how it is useful.
   - Elicit the highest positive intention of that part (chunk up).
   - Thank the part for this positive intention.

3. **Place other part in other hand and make it 'real'.**
   - Create a visual, auditory and kinaesthetic representation for the part in that hand, or select a suitable object.
   - Ask this part what resources and strengths it brings – how it is useful.
   - Elicit the highest positive intention of that part (chunk up).
   - Thank the part for this positive intention.

4. *Ask each part if it could learn anything from the other part.*
   - Allow each part to explain to the other part how and in what ways it is of benefit to the person.
   - Ask each part if it has other ways to serve the same purpose that do not conflict.
   - Thank each part for cooperating so well.

5. *Bring parts slowly together*
   - When the persons hands join ask if the two parts would like to become one new and different part or would they prefer to co-exist with greater knowledge and wisdom.

6. *Bring new part(s) to the chest and incorporate into the body.*

7. *Ecology check*
   - Ask if there are any other parts that object to this new arrangement. If 'yes' go through the process again with the parts concerned.

8. *Generalise and Future pace*
   - *"I want you to go out into the future to a time when you have experienced the results of your new learnings. How are things different now? Go to another situation, OK? Go to another situation, OK? Go to as many future situations as you need. When you are ready, come back to now."*

9. *What is the next smallest step that will help you move in the direction you want to go?*

7

Motivation

"No longer conscious of my movement, I discovered a new unity with nature. I had found a new source of power and beauty, a source I never dreamt existed."

Roger Bannister

ELEMENTS OF MOTIVATION

Motivation is a key theme in coaching. Clients often describe a lack of motivation as the cause for not carrying out the behaviours they want to, as in *"I want to make 5 new sales calls each week but I'm just not motivated to do it"*. Sometimes your client will have considered the situation and cause thoroughly and will have identified motivation as their required coaching outcome *"I want to be motivated to complete a marathon"*. When increasing motivation is a solution to the client's current problem there are 4 key areas for investigation and change - state, meta programs, values and beliefs.

> *"The most important thing in changing human behaviour is the person's motivation"*
>
> *Milton Erickson*

State

- Motivation is an emotional state and you can use a memory to construct the state to use as a resource. Think of a time when you were motivated in the way you want to be now. What was it in the past situation that got you motivated? How did you maintain that motivation? How can you create that state now? Can you adopt the physiology and breathing pattern you had at the time? What happens if you see what you saw, hear what you heard and feel what you felt? How is this state helpful to you now? Anchor the state!

Meta Programs

- Meta-programs are unconscious filtering systems that direct the habitual ways we gather information, make decisions and responses and evaluate situations. For instance, in your career do you tend to like stability and commonality (sameness) or new and uniqueness (difference)? People tend to be motivated by things that fit with their preferred meta programs.

Values

- Values define what is important to us and are the basis for how we evaluate the events we experience. They are generally the things that we move towards (like success, achievement, harmony, power or freedom) or away from (like failure, arguments, weakness or restriction). People are naturally motivated when their desired actions fit with a congruent set of personal values.

Beliefs

- Beliefs tend to filter those things that we can/can't or will/won't do. They have a direct effect on behaviour and shape our perceptions of the world – if we believe that something is a certain way then we will filter our experiences to prove to ourselves that it is so. Ensuring a person has resourceful beliefs will allow them to approach life with the freedom to go after and get whatever they truly want.

The Expectancy – Value Theory of Motivation

The Expectancy-Value theory from Feather (1982) says that motivation in learning is a combination of a persons desire (their values) multiplied by their expectations (their beliefs).

When you want to motivate an individual or group to carry out some action (perhaps a complete a task) include elements to move away from and move towards, and build a positive outcome expectancy. Some values and beliefs you could include:

Values

To move away from
- Failure
- Loneliness
- Powerlessness

and move towards
- Success and achievement
- Positive relationships
- Influence and control

Beliefs
- It is possible
- It is achievable
- They are capable
- It's desirable
- They deserve the rewards

Procrastination

Procrastination typically occurs when there is a mismatch between a person's desire and their expectations. For example, if a person wants to run a marathon but doesn't believe they will be able to do the training they will put off starting. Another reason people delay starting is when they are doing things for other people's reasons, not their own. Two key questions for any behaviour or action:

- What personal value does it help you meet?
- What makes you sure you can do it?

Types of Motivation

Being motivated is a process not an event and there are many different ways to feel motivated including a high energy, bouncing around, up for it motivation; a style of inner calm, focus, determination and drive; and many others in between. Remember your clients version of motivation will be different to yours or anyone else's.

- What type of motivation does your client need in their current situation?
- What is the most appropriate way for you to help your client build their motivation?

META-PROGRAMS

Meta programs are the deepest unconscious filters we have on our perceptions and behaviours. Meta programs represent our preferred way of doing things in a particular context.

By understanding some of the meta programs related to motivation you can appreciate your natural preference, and how others may operate differently. Several helpful meta programs for coaches to be aware of are:

What is your motivational direction?

How you think about your goals indicates how you get motivated to achieve your goals. What drives all your actions? What drives the way you think, act and behave? Are you motivated away-from pain or towards pleasure?

- What is important to you at work (or home or interests)?

Towards people will tell you what do they want to achieve; *"This order will help us increase sales and raise salaries". "In the future I would like to have a wonderful house and to earn a lot of money."*

Away-from people will tell what they want to avoid; *"This order will help us to avoid the crisis and the being ousted by the competition". "In the future I don't want to live on this estate and be unemployed."*

Implications for coaching

Is your motivation for coaching to help people find solutions or avoid problems? An away-from motivation can be a very effective kick start to action but tends to reduce the further away the person moves from the motivation source. A towards motivation is usually most effective supporting in a dynamic situation where progress has begun in the direction of the desired goal(s).

What is the source of your motivation?

Do you find motivation in **external** sources or **internal** standards and beliefs?

- How do you know if you've done a good job?

Internal reference people are motivated by their own internal standards. They measure against internal references to know how well they are doing.

External reference people require outside feedback to keep them motivated. They measure how well they are doing by external feedback and the opinions of others.

Implications for coaching

What is your split between internal and external reference as a coach? Too much internal reference and a person may not ask for or pay attention to valuable information from others. Too much focus on external reference can reduce a person's trust in themselves and their own perceptions and abilities.

What is your motivational reason?

How do you approach your daily life and work? Do you continually look for new **options** and ways to do it or do you prefer to stick to established **procedures**?

- Why did you choose your current career (or house or phone)?

Options people are motivated by choices and opportunities. They are good at creating new procedures but hate to follow them - they like to search for different ways to do things. Give an options person a guaranteed way to make a million pounds and they will try to improve it.

Procedures people prefer to follow set routines and ways. They prefer established procedures and methods. They believe there is a right way to do things and without a procedure they may feel lost. They feel compelled to complete what they start.

Implications for coaching

How does your preference for options or procedures impact on the style and approach you have as a coach? An options client may need challenging in order to stop generating new options and decide on how they will carry out the specific actions. A procedures client may be challenged when they can't predict and plan for everything and has to keep their options open.

What factors influence your decisions?

How do you react to change? Do prefer things to be familiar and look for **sameness** or are you attracted by **difference** and the new and unique?

- What is the relationship between this year and last year?

Sameness people are motivated by similarity and matching experience *"it's still the same; I keep things going round here."* They look for what is in common and may accept major change once every 10 years.

Difference people often mismatch the present (yes, but...) and resist static or stable situations *"it's totally different now my promotion has been confirmed."* They usually need a major change every 1-2 years.

Implications for coaching

How does your preference for sameness or difference impact on your coaching syle? A client with a sameness preference will often benefit from using their past as a useful source for options and resources. A client with a difference preference may discount their existing knowledge in order to focus on reinventing the wheel. How new does it need to be?

What level of information do you prefer?

Do you naturally pay attention to **general** information or prefer to talk about the **specifics** of a situation?

- What information do you need when asking for directions?

General people often filter for and talk about general concepts and give an overview of *"the big picture."* They often want to discuss *"what is really important"* and will accept ideas in a random order.

Specific people prefer to talk and filter information in a step by step manner with lots of detail *"yesterday I met with my boss and passed him a report I'd written about how we could improve efficiency in the front office when responding to new enquiries."*

Implications for coaching

How does your preference for general or specific impact on how you listen to your client? Chunking up and down is an effecive way to shift between different levels of information. Clients with a general preference often benefit from being challenged on the specifics of what, where and when. Specific people can get caught in the details and lose motivation unless they connect to the bigger picture of what they are doing.

Where do you normally place your attention?

Do you naturally pay attention to the behaviour of **others** or is your focus on your**self** and your own experience?

- What is the most important aspect of communication?

Self people tend to focus on the content of what others say and their own internal experiences. Though they are aware of their feelings they may not show many emotions and will focus on what they are doing. They tend to take decisions based on their own interests.

Other people are influenced by rapport and the responses they conscious or unconsciously observe in others. In communication they are often animated and respond to others gestures and facial expressions. They tend to focus on the needs and activities of others.

Implications for coaching

The ability to operate with an other preference is a essential skilll for coaches in order to build effective rapport. Communicating with a self person requires well structured arguments or explanations.Too much focus on self can lead to a person missing information and an inability to pick up the cues that lead to effective rapport. Too much focus on other can lead to paying less attention to the technical or specific content the person is communicating.

Coaching with Meta Programs

Meta programs represent preferences for taking in and filtering information. As coaches our meta programs influence our coaching practice and may lie behind the experience of coaches who find they have a better 'fit' with some clients or organisations than others. The ability to operate across the full range of meta programs both for yourself as a coach and for your clients will provide greater choice and freedom in the options available to achieve goals.

NLP has described over 60 different meta program patterns, some of which are more useful than others. It is important to remember that we have the ability to use all preferences at certain times; your meta program preference is not an excuse!

- People can often be stuck operating in their preferred meta programs
- Operating with a different set of meta programs provides new information
- People are naturally motivated to take action in line with their meta programs
- Bringing meta programs to a person's awareness can give them choice over their internal processing and behaviour
- Deliberate practice can make a meta program preference feel more natural and effortless

Contrasting Meta Programs

1. *Identify a situation where you have had difficulty making a decision, being motivated or solving a problem.*

2. *Associate fully to the experience and identify the meta programs you are using in the present situation.*

Towards	Internal	Options	Sameness	General	Self
Away-from	External	Procedures	Difference	Specific	Other

3. *Think of a similar situation in which you successfully made a decision, were motivated or solved a problem. Associate fully to the experience and identify the meta programs you used in that successful situation.*

Towards	Internal	Options	Sameness	General	Self
Away-from	External	Procedures	Difference	Specific	Other

4. *Contrast the two experiences. How are the meta programs different?*

5. *Step back into the present state bringing with you those meta programs that give you more information, options or choice in the desired situation? Associate fully to holding these new resources.*

6. *What is the next smallest step that will take you in a helpful direction?*

WORKING WITH VALUES

Values are what are important to us and are those things that a person is willing to invest time, energy and resources to achieve or avoid. They are the things we move toward or away from and drive a person's true purpose as a human being; they influence all of our behaviour. We are aware of some of our values at a conscious level. The core values that direct and influence how we live and work are more likely to be at the unconscious level.

Higher Intention

A useful presupposition of NLP states that *"every behaviour is directed by a positive intention for that person, given their map of the world"*. Often the higher intention or purpose behind a particular behaviour is meeting a core value. The behaviour a person engages in represents the best choice the person has (in that situation, at that moment in time) to meet their value(s) or avoid compromising them.

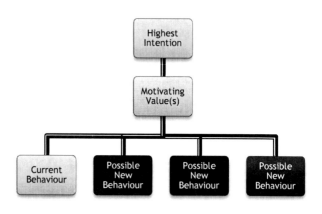

For a person to be motivated to change behaviour, the new behaviour they want to engage in must be connected to their personal value system and aligned with their higher intention. If it does not then they will be unlikely to carry out the behaviour, no matter how much they think it's a good idea or that they should be doing it. It is much easier to align change with people's natural motivational flow than attempt to change it.

Adding Behavioural Choice

1. *What behaviour would you like to change?*

2. *What is your highest intention in carrying out this behaviour?*
   Help the person reveal their values and intention held at an unconscious level.

3. *What are at least three other options you could take that would meet this higher intention at least as well or even better than the old behaviour?*

4. *Which of the options, or set of options, will you now choose to use?*
   Ensure there is a congruent commitment to using the new behaviours.

5. *Are there any other changes that need to be made?*

6. *What is the next smallest step that will take you in a helpful direction?*

Discovering Intention & Motivating Values

Values are a process not a thing, though we often refer to them as if they were. They represent a preference for what we like and are usually quite general concepts. The use of several chunking-up questions with a person often takes them to the level of values.

- For what purpose do you want _____?
- What's important to you about_____?
- What will having _____ give you?

For example:	
What do you want?	To work with my manager more effectively
For what purpose do you want to <u>work with your manager more effectively</u>?	To get greater **harmony.**
What's important to you about <u>greater harmony</u>?	I get to **achieve** my goals.
For what purpose do you want to <u>achieve your goals</u>?	To be **successful.**

Building Motivation and making a Suggestion

Once the motivating values have been identified you can link them to a general suggestion that helps the client move in a helpful direction. This could be building motivation for the coaching session, setting up the next stage of the coaching process, for actually taking their next smallest step or living their life with freedom and choice.

- So in order to get _____ and _____,
  (outcome)   *(values)*
  would you be willing to _____?
  (suggestion)

For example:
So in order to work <u>with your manager more effectively</u> and enable you to <u>get greater harmony, achieve your goals and be successful</u>, would you be willing to <u>discover new ways to communicate</u>?
So in order to <u>have fun, laugh lots</u> and <u>get respect</u>, would you be willing to <u>take full responsibility for your actions during this programme</u>?

CHOICES AND DECISIONS

Values drive our decisions and provide motivation before we take action, are the way we judge good and bad, right and wrong.

Values have a significant impact on our emotional state and provide the motives for behaviours explained by phrases like *"It seemed the decent thing to do"*, or *"I did it because I want to live with myself in peace"*.

- Coaching can help people explore (and change) their value system
- Effective coaching helps people make decisions in line with their value system

> *"We all subconsciously use values. We "look" at the world—people, products, concepts, events—and instantly decide to accept or reject. Things are either good/or bad, right/or wrong, normal/or not normal. Only if something's purely functional like a pencil or a screwdriver can we be neutral. But when human feelings are involved, and feelings are there every time we interact...then values guide us."*
>
> Morris Massey
> *(What You Are Is Where You Were When - AGAIN! 2005)*

Sources of Values

Since we all have a different social background and personal history we have evolved our own unique set of values. Some of the key influences to values occur in our childhood and include family, friends, church or religion, school / teachers, geography / location, economics / prosperity, music and television, major historical events and significant personal emotional events.

Exploring our values gives us choice over how we use them.

- Which of your values did you learn from your family and growing up?
- Which of your values did you learn from friends and social interests?
- Which of your values did you learn from your work?
- Which of your values are still current and serve you well?
- Which of your values are out of date and no longer serve you well?

Hierarchy of Values

We tend to have a number of values that are important to us and arrange them in a hierarchy or importance. By knowing your own personal hierarchy you can make effective decisions that fit your needs.

In teams people will often behave quite differently because even though they may share similar values, each person's unique meaning and hierarchy will motivate their behaviour in different ways. Identifying a common values hierarchy with a team can provide a sound base for consistent decision making and effective future planning.

Making Choices

The first stage of making any choice is to gather information. In communication sensory grounded information is of the highest possible quality. In other areas memories, thoughts, intuitions and experience can play a greater role. A person's meta-program preference influences the information they will pay attention to. For a well rounded decision ensure a person gathers information using the full range of meta-programs.

Values provide the hidden criteria by which we explore the choices available and make decisions. In a world of ever expanding choice, where more options are seen as the key to freedom, having a sound basis on which to evaluate the choices available is essential. Coaching can help people who don't know the criteria they are using to make choices, haven't evaluated whether the criteria are serving them well and haven't chosen the criteria that fit their desired outcomes for the future.

Consider the differing outcomes that might result when a person makes a choice using the following values as selection criteria:

Possible criteria for selecting a meal at a restaurant:	Possible criteria for selecting between two plans of action	Possible criteria for choosing a particular coaching intervention:
Cost Immediate pleasure How you will feel tomorrow Steady energy release Balanced food groups Fitting in with others New or different Familiar	Shortest time to implement Easiest to implement Long term impact People/equipment needed Level of staff training needed Alignment with vision Quick return Overall cost	Time available Have done it before Haven't done it before It worked on me It has worked before Easiest to run Develops my coaching skill Generative for the client

When a person's or group's desired outcome and their selection criteria are congruent then they are likely to move closer to getting the results they desire in life. Whenever they don't match then inner conflict, indecision or dissatisfaction is likely. Effective teams share a common value set for decision making. Questions to explore a decision include:

- What is your big picture outcome for this decision?
- What values or criteria are you using to evaluate your options?
- Is this set of values supporting you to get the outcomes you desire?
- Would applying different values or criteria serve you even better?
- How will this new set of values support you and others in the future?

MOTIVATION USING HIGHER VALUES

Since some things are more important than others, we unconsciously arrange values in hierarchies. Motivation at work often comes when a person's values are compatible with the values that are in operation in their team at work. Motivation in life comes when a person has balance in their work, interests and relationships that meets their value system.

People usually don't take action, even though they know they want to when there is a limiting value that stops them. For instance *"I want to go running more regularly because it would be good for my fitness only I don't like going out in the rain and feeling cold."* By going beyond the limiting value to a higher or core value it is possible to build a stronger lasting motivation for a new behaviour by meeting the needs of the core values. *"I'd be willing to run more regularly because it would be good for my fitness and even though I don't like going out in the rain and sometimes feeling chilly, it is more important for me to be able to perform at my best and make my family proud of me."*

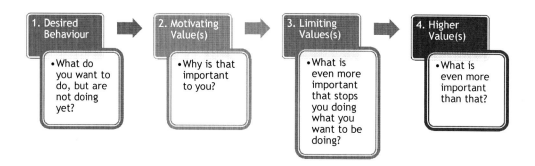

Values Ladder Technique

This process is based on Robert Dilts Hierarchy of Criteria Technique and works very well if you get your client to physically move through the four positions. First, ensure your client has identified a specific behaviour they want to build greater motivation for like exercise consistently, spend time with the family, complete the monthly reports, etc.

1. ***Step into position 1 - "What do you want to do but are not doing yet?"***
    Define the specific behaviour your client wants to do but is not doing yet.
    *   E.g. "I want to <u>complete my reports</u> each week"

2. ***Step into Position 2 - "Why is that important to you?"***
    Identify the value(s) that motivate your client to want the behaviour.
    *   E.g. "To be <u>efficient</u> and <u>to please</u> my boss"

3. *Step into Position 3 – "What is even more important that stops you doing what you to be doing?"*
    Identify the values that stop your client from carrying out the behaviour in the way they want to.
    - *E.g. "No _time_, not very _interesting_ - I like _starting new_ projects, "*

4. *Step into Position 4 – "What is even more important than that?"*
    Identify the higher value(s) that override the limiting value - what would they always make time for?
    - *E.g. "Taking care of _my family_, being _true to myself_"*

5. *Step back into position 1 and combine the higher value with the desired behaviour*
    - *E.g. "Could you be _true to yourself_ and _complete your reports_ in order to _take care of your family_?"*

6. *Step back into position 2 and combine motivating and higher values*
    - *E.g. "See yourself _being efficient_ and _completing your reports_ which means that you are able to _be true to yourself_, _please your boss_ and _take care of your family_. Feel good about it"*

7. *Step back into position 3 – Collapse the limiting criteria by applying the motivating and higher values together and ask the client for a new solution.*
    - *E.g. "Is there some _new_ and _interesting_ way of _completing your reports_ that doesn't take much _time_ and which allows you to know your _boss_ _will be pleased_ and your _family are cared for_ as you do it?"*

8. *Repeat through as many cycles as you need using different combinations of the client's words. When change happens your client will have shifted state and will probably have discovered a new way to carry out their desired behaviour that meets all their values.*

9. *What is the next smallest step that will take you in a helpful direction?*

BELIEF SYSTEMS

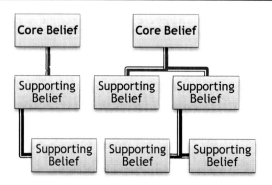

Beliefs are those convictions we trust as being true. They are statements about our internal representations or how we believe the world is. They are generalisations about our actions and about what we are doing and about what we want to do. Beliefs are attached or related to a certain values in clusters and may form a Belief System.

Beliefs Describe Relationships

Belief statements are concerned with the relationships between things, not the things themselves. They are composed of judgements, causes, meanings and comparisons etc. A complete belief statement has three elements – a cause, an effect and a meaning. For example *"If I work hard I'll make a lot of money which means I'm a successful person."*

Sometimes your client may make a full belief statement *"If I study like my parents told me I'll get good grades but it still won't be good enough"* but most commonly they will express the final meaning *"I am a successful person"* or *"it'll never be good enough."*

- Establishing a full belief statement by asking *"How do you know that?"* and *"What makes it that way?"* is the first step to working with beliefs.

When We Believe Something, We Act As If It Is True.

Beliefs are learned and they can be added to or changed. In my coaching experience I have come across four different categories of beliefs:

Empowering Beliefs	Neutral Beliefs	Limiting Beliefs	Core Beliefs
Beliefs that support and positively influence behaviour and learning from experience. Building empowering beliefs helps people to perform to their potential.	*Beliefs that neither help nor hinder. Consider turning neutral beliefs into empowering beliefs or put them in your museum of old beliefs.*	*Beliefs that lead to hesitation, reluctance fear and doubt. Changing limiting beliefs can transform a person's level of performance.*	*Beliefs that shape identity, behaviour and the way a person lives their life. Core beliefs often operate at an unconscious level.*

Empowering Belief Systems

A belief system is a network of connected beliefs that support or limit behaviour in certain ways. For example a manager or sportsman with a positive belief system allows them to celebrate each success to the full and see any failure as feedback from which to develop even more.

An unhelpful belief system around a topic can limit or even stop progress towards the goal, like a boat having something caught around its propeller will prevent it moving forward effectively. Some people often have complex belief systems around success, health, exercise or learning that need addressing as a whole for behaviour to change.

Five Empowering Beliefs to Hold

Deserving	Capable	Possible	Appropriate	Desirable
• Only you can decide if you are worthy of achieving your goals, but why not? You are as entitled as everyone else in the world to succeed at what you desire aren't you? **You deserve to achieve**	• Have you put a mental block on achievements? Do you sell yourself short ? You have not yet reached the limit of what you are capable of, have you? **You are able to achieve**	• We often mistake possibility for competence. You cannot know what your limits are until you reach them. You can't not do something, you just haven't done it... yet. **It is possible to achieve**	• Do you think success is for others and high goals are beyond your reach? That is just not true.It is appropriate for you to have as much success as anyone else isn't it? **You should achieve**	• Have you given yourself permission to consider what it is you really want? Let your creative mind loose with possibility and be free to want what you truly desire. **You want to achieve**

Time Shifting Beliefs

In general use your language to put problems and limiting beliefs in the past; resources and empowering beliefs in the present; and the positive consequences of changes made in the future. Using time shifted belief statements makes a powerful affirmation when used with a person or group in an altered state. For example:

> *"In the past you may have thought that some things were not possible for you, or your skills and abilities were not as great as they really are. In fact even though some people didn't used to think they deserve or desire success, they can realise, now, that they are as entitled as anyone to achieving what they truly want. By knowing and trusting your-self you can explore beyond the limits of your capability to discover what is truly possible and how great you really are."*

BUILDING OR EXPLORING A BELIEF

Beliefs don't just magically appear, we usually believe something if we have a good reason to believe it. Robert Dilts has suggested the basic types of underlying causes or reasons for believing something defined by Aristotle can be revealed by using certain connective words. He offers this example; to discover a reason to believe that *"Ghandi was an effective leader"* following the statement with the word *"because"* can lead to the conclusion: *"Gandhi was an effective leader **because** he congruently embodied his vision and mission through his actions."*

Using the 9 connective words allows a coach to help a client explore or 'audit' the various 'causes' related to a particular belief. By breaking the belief into smaller elements they become easier change or strengthen. The belief becomes in the control of your client.

In coaching you can either help your client:

- Explore a limiting belief   or   Build an empowering belief

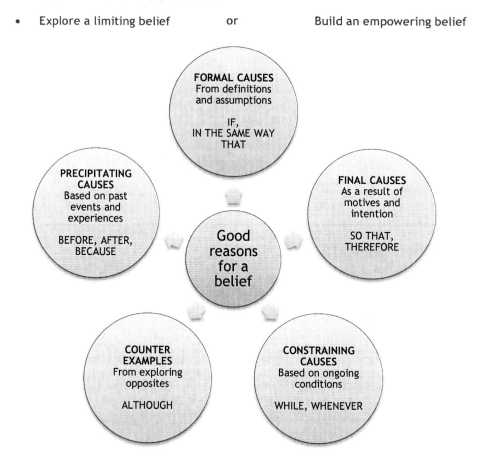

Exploring a Belief

Specific Belief _____

I / We hold this to be true....

Because	
Therefore	
After	
While	
Whenever	
So that	
If	
Although	
In the same way that	

When all the connectives have been completed for a positive belief they can create a powerful and motivating speech which is very powerful if you read back to your client when they are in an altered state. For example:

> *"I am a skilled NLP coach <u>because</u> I have practiced what I know <u>therefore</u> I can tell if what I'm doing is working <u>after</u> high quality training. **I am a skilled NLP coach** <u>while</u> with my clients <u>whenever</u> I choose to be <u>so that</u> I can help people fulfil their potential <u>if</u> I remember to be in the right state <u>although</u> sometimes it takes a little while. **I am a skilled NLP coach** <u>in the same way that</u> I am skilled at my work."*

ASSESSING BELIEFS ABOUT A GOAL

On the 6th May 1954 Roger Bannister completed a feat that some members of the sporting world did not believe was possible and within the field of human endurance. When Bannister became the first person to run a mile in less than 4 minutes his actions inspired many people to change their belief about what was possible for them.

In 1952 Bannister's closest rival John Landy came close with 4:02.1 but declared *"Frankly, I think the four-minute mile is beyond my capabilities. Two seconds may not sound much, but to me it's like trying to break through a brick wall. Someone may achieve the four-minute mile the world is wanting so badly, but I don't think I can."* 46 Days after Roger Bannister ran the mile in 3:59.4 John Landy ran the mile in 3:57.0

A person's expectations and beliefs link their behaviour and the outcomes they seek.

- **Self-efficacy** represents the belief a person has in their ability to perform the behaviours needed to achieve their goals. If a person believes they can perform certain behaviours they are likely to create a plan that uses those behaviours to get the outcomes they want.
- **Outcome expectancy** is the belief that if a person engages in certain behaviours then they will lead to their desired outcome. A strong outcome expectancy will lead to someone taking the steps required to execute their plan.

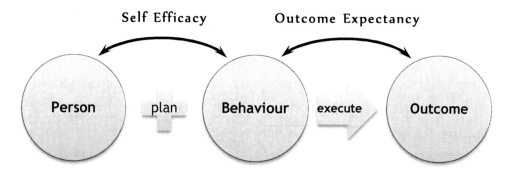

Robert Dilts has identified five key beliefs that support this process.

1. The Outcome is desirable
2. The Behaviour is possible
3. The Behaviour is appropriate
4. The Person is capable of carrying out the behaviour
5. The Person deserves to achieve the outcome

Belief Self Assessment

Take the time to really consider how you truly feel about a goal. Rate your own personal strength of belief in yourself to achieve your goal, where ❶ is only just believe and ❺ represents 100% definite self belief.

My Goal
(Be specific and positive) _____

	Just believe	Mostly believe	I believe	Confidently believe	Absolutely believe
I deserve to achieve my goal and am responsible for doing it	①	②	③	④	⑤
I am capable of doing what I need to do to achieve my goal	①	②	③	④	⑤
It is possible to achieve my goal	①	②	③	④	⑤
I believe achieving my goal is appropriate for me to do	①	②	③	④	⑤
I truly want to achieve my goal	①	②	③	④	⑤

Reflect on the reasons you gave the scores you did.

- What makes each belief assessment as high as it is?
- What could you do to increase your strength of belief in each area?
- Who could mentor and support you with each belief?

BUILDING SELF-EFFICACY

Self efficacy is a belief in your ability to achieve your chosen tasks and goals in life. Albert Bandura discovered that a high level of self efficacy helps people deal with the unexpected and learn more effectively. *"People with high assurance in their capabilities approach difficult tasks as challenges to be mastered rather than as threats to be avoided."* (*Encyclopaedia of Human Behaviour*, 1994).

People with a weak sense of self-efficacy	People with a strong sense of self-efficacy
• Avoid challenging tasks • Believe that difficult tasks and situations are beyond their capabilities • Focus on personal failings and negative outcomes • Quickly lose confidence in personal abilities	• View challenging problems as tasks to be mastered • Develop deeper interest in the activities in which they participate • Form a stronger sense of commitment to their interests and activities • Recover quickly from setbacks and disappointments

Self Efficacy and Performance

A strong sense of self efficacy is also essential in the process of improving performance. Robert Dilts has illustrated how it plays a part in the four stages of learning & improving skills outlined by US Gordon Training International (& others).

1. Initially, we are pleased to discover we have more skills than expected, and we **"know more than we think"** (*unconscious competence*)

2. As skills develop we feel good about ourselves, but we **"don't know what we don't know"** (*unconscious incompetence*)

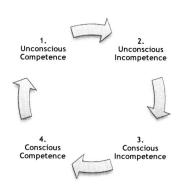

3. When we become aware that **"we know we don't know"** (*conscious incompetence*) our performance takes a natural dip. If a person gets disappointed at this point of greatest difference between expected and actual performance then they may revise their expectations *"It was too hard for me"* or *"I shouldn't have expected so much"* as it appears the easier option at that time. A person who maintains a strong self-efficacy and learns new strategies as they go through the trial and error process will develop their skills and improve their performance.

4. As performance increases we **"know we know"** (*conscious competence*), we move towards a higher level of unconscious competence and the cycle restarts.

Typical effect of low self belief on performance

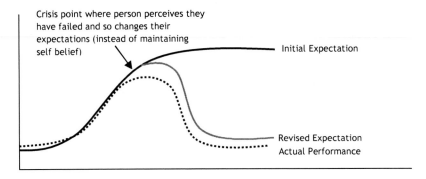

Crisis point where person perceives they have failed and so changes their expectations (instead of maintaining self belief)

Initial Expectation

Revised Expectation
Actual Performance

Typical effect of **high self belief** on performance

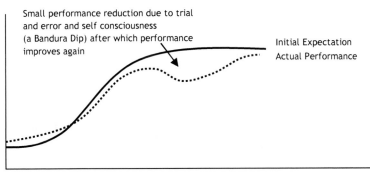

Small performance reduction due to trial and error and self consciousness (a Bandura Dip) after which performance improves again

Initial Expectation
Actual Performance

Developing Self Efficacy

A coaching conversation is an excellent way to discuss how a person can build a strong sense of belief in their abilities. Discussing in advance where a person might experience a 'Bandura Dip' be can help them focus on the approaches they can use to improve their performance. Albert Bandura identified 4 main ways to develop self-efficacy:

Build a positive set of reference experiences from your history of failure and success
Learn from others meeting the same sorts of challenges
Select a mentor - someone who will help and encourage you
Develop your emotional maturity and manage emotional states

IDENTIFYING & CHANGING BELIEFS

Beliefs are inherited or formed as generalisation about how the world is at a certain point in time. The generalisation is helpful to keep us safe, make sense of a situation or achieve the results we want in a specific context. Useful beliefs that continue to serve us are empowering beliefs.

> *"A person is as he believes"*
>
> *Anton Chekhov*

Limiting beliefs are those things a person believes about themselves that place limitations on their abilities. The person never gets to find out what their potential is in a particular area of work or life because a limiting belief stops them, sometimes before they even start. Limitations are a mental construct.

- Limiting beliefs are helpful beliefs that are out of date.

Identifying Limiting Beliefs

Beliefs are often hidden in the language your client uses. You can identify them by listening carefully as a coach and asking yourself *"what does a person have to believe in order to make that statement?"* Check your intuition with the client and listen for the assumptions behind the answers to a question like *"what stops you achieving your goal?"*

Conducting a belief audit and / or exploring building self efficacy may reveal a limiting belief. Some examples of limiting beliefs are:

Examples	Can indicate limiting beliefs about
I can't change, I never remember facts, I can't do any more, we don't have the skills, they did all they could	Capability
It won't work, it's impossible, we tried before and failed, you can't do that on this machine, it simply can't be done	Possibility
I shouldn't be here, we don't deserve it, it's not for people like us, I'm not worth it, someone else can collect the award	Deserving
I can't have fun at work, we shouldn't do that, it's just not how librarians act, they shouldn't go out looking like that	Appropriateness
It's not my goal, it's not important, the targets are just numbers on a spreadsheet, I don't want it anyway	Desirability

Beliefs aren't fixed, they represent an active process of believing and can be adopted, changed or let go if you make up your mind to do it. Determination always finds a way around obstacles – where there's a will there's a way and where there's a way there can be a will.

Changing beliefs

Changing a belief involves expanding the current map of the world for a person or a group. Preparation is the key to successfully helping someone change their beliefs. Help the person consider all the consequences of change.

Exploring the Belief

By bringing the belief to the person's awareness you are empowering them to look at it from an outside perspective and consider whether it is useful or not. This can be a very helpful process for exploring neutral beliefs.

- What have you been believing until now?
- How long have you been believing this?
- What have been the benefits of believing this?
- Are you absolutely sure that it is true?
- How would you know if the old belief was no longer true?
- What would be the benefits of believing something different?

The Belief Change Process

Robert Dilts likens the natural process of belief change to the cyclical process of the changing of the seasons.

When we stop believing something we currently believe, we first become open to doubting it (is Father Christmas real or just my Dad?). After recognising that the belief no longer serves us, it becomes an old belief in our 'Museum of Personal History' as something we used to believe back then.

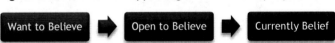

Currently Believe ➡ Open to Doubt ➡ Old Belief

When we want to believe something, first we must be open to believing it. This is an exciting phase and a strong outcome and set of supporting beliefs will help a person to shift the new belief from open to believe to currently believe.

Want to Believe ➡ Open to Believe ➡ Currently Belief

A coaching conversation that helps a person move through the process of change from a state of inner trust and congruence will enable them to explore their current beliefs, make any adjustments needed to build empowering beliefs and move old beliefs to their 'Museum of Personal History'.

Reframing the Belief

Use the reframing patterns to help a person change the meaning behind what they are saying. Sometimes a well placed reframe will enable a person to immediately transform their belief. Often, reframing is a useful tool to help people to achieve the Open to Believe or Open to Doubt states in the Belief Change process.

BELIEF CHANGE CYCLE

This technique from Robert Dilts eliminates the effect of a limiting belief that your client may have been holding and increases confidence in going into the future with a set of new and empowering beliefs.

1.   *Identify the belief or belief system you want to hold or hold more strongly*

2.   *Create specific spatial anchors by stepping onto each location and fully connecting with the associated state.* (You are not thinking about the specific beliefs to change at this stage, just setting the states up)

- *Want to Believe*
  Remember a time when there was something you really wanted to believe (reaching a goal).

- *Open to Believe*
  Remember a time when you were open and excited to adopt a new belief (I can drive).

- *Currently Believe*
  What is it like when you believe or know something to be true (the sun will rise)?

- *Open to Doubt*
  Remember a time when you were open to doubt something that you had believed up until that time (Father Christmas).

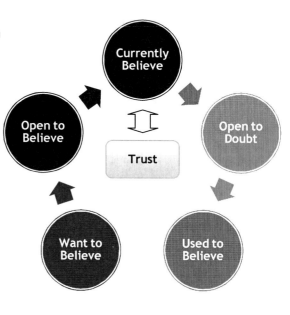

- *Used to Believe*
  Remember several beliefs that you used to believe but no longer believe. What beliefs have you got in your "Museum of Personal History?" (The Tooth Fairy).

- *Trust*
  Remember a situation of deep personal trust, perhaps a time when you didn't know what to think of believe anymore and you just had to trust in yourself and what was happening.

3. *Move round the Belief Change Cycle*

Walk the person round the cycle, encouraging them to fully connect with the thoughts and feelings of each position as they consider their beliefs at each stage. Use reframing, different perceptual positions (what would a trusted mentor advise?) and higher intention where appropriate to help a person shift their beliefs. The process can be completed in one exercise or over a period of time when on a walk for example.

1. **Stand in 'want to believe'**
Think of the belief that you wish to have more confidence in. Prepare to step into the 'open to believe' space with this belief in mind.

2. **Step into 'open to believe'**
Feel what it is like to being more open to believe this new belief. When you intuitively feel the time is appropriate step into the 'currently believe' space.

3. **Step into 'currently believe'**
If there are any conflicting or limiting beliefs that come up in the currently believe space, hold them in your mind and move to the 'trust' space.

4. **Step into 'trust'**
Consider the positive intent and purpose of the new belief and any conflicting beliefs. See if there are any adjustments you wish to make to the new belief. Consider if there are any parts of the old belief you want to keep.

5. **Step into 'open to doubt'**
Bring your insights from the 'trust' space and prepare to move any conflicting or limiting beliefs into the 'used to believe' space.

6. **Step into 'used to believe'**
Store away any conflicting or limiting beliefs into your "museum of personal history." See them in a labelled box on the shelf next to other old beliefs. Remember if you ever want them again in the future, you can get them back.

7. **Stand in 'want to believe'**
Are there any other new beliefs you want or need to support you now?

8. **Step into 'open to believe'**
What will it be like to hold these new beliefs - are they something you really want?

9. **Step into 'currently believe'**
Enjoy the feeling of the new beliefs integrating with all your other beliefs.

10. **Step into 'trust'**
Use the trust space to look at your current beliefs with the new belief in place. Are there any other adjustments needed?

11. **Go round the cycle again as many times as you need to**

12. **Step out of the cycle**
Experience being yourself with this new belief set. What will you do that you didn't do before? What will your future be like?

TIMELINE BELIEF CHANGE PROCESS

A timeline is an excellent way to assist a person to change a past limiting belief like *"it's not possible to do this"* or *"I'm not capable of doing it"*, and replace it with a new empowering belief. The process is written for you to take your client through as they physically walk their timeline – you can invite clients to use a pattern in the carpet or the space between some trees in the local park to represent their past, present and future.

1. **Have a clear and agreed outcome for the process**
   - *"What is the belief that limits you in this particular context?"*

   - This process is ideally suited **for beliefs about capability, possibility or desirability.** For significant traumatic experiences or events I suggest you refer your client to a suitably qualified psychotherapist.

   - *"Are you willing to change this unhelpful belief from the past for something more useful now?"*

2. **Find the earliest event**
   - *"What was the root cause, the earliest event where the unhelpful belief was formed? If you were to know, what age were you?"*

3. **Ask the person to imagine their timeline on the floor in front of them. Locate now on the timeline, and the direction of the past and the future.**

4. **Walk back along the timeline and look down on the earliest event**
   - *"Now, walk back alongside the timeline to age ___, directly above the event so that you are looking down on the event."*

5. **Collect the learnings**
   - *"Step further away from the timeline and look down on the younger you going through that event. Ask your unconscious what it needs to learn from the event, the learning of which will allow you to let go of the unhelpful belief easily and effortlessly."* (Pause and wait for learnings)

   - *"Are the learnings positive and useful to you?"* (If no, ask for more learnings)

   - *"Is there anything else to learn? Anything else?"* (Check you have all the learnings)

   - *"Store the learnings in the place you store such learnings so that if you need them in the future, they'll be there."*

6. **Walk before event and check the old belief has gone**
    - *"Now walk back further to before the earliest event so that you are looking toward now. Ask yourself, now, where is the old belief? Is it there or has it gone?"*
    - If the limiting belief has gone (it will have if they were at the earliest event), carry on to the next step. If the limiting belief is still there ask the person to go back to an even earlier event and continue from step 5.

7. **If appropriate, insert an empowering and useful new belief**
    - *"If appropriate, what belief would be more empowering, useful and appropriate for the younger you to hold in that situation? Choose an inspiring belief that serves both the younger you back then and the older you right now."*
    - *"See the younger you holding the new belief."*

8. **Experience the event in a new way**
    - *"Step onto your timeline and inside the event, looking through your own eyes and re-experience it differently. What emotions are present instead?"*

9. **Come back to now**
    - *"Now step off the timeline and see the younger you holding a new belief. In a moment, walk back to now looking down on your timeline and noticing how your memories realign themselves. Come all the way back to the present and preserve all the learnings. Ready, go!"*
    - Wait until person is done

10. **Generalise and Future Pace**
    - *"I want you to walk out into the future to a time when you have experienced the results of your new learnings and new belief. How are things different now? Good, go to another situation, OK? Good, go to another situation, OK? Good. Go to as many future situations as you need. When you are ready, come back to now bringing all your learnings with you."*

11. **What is your next step that will take you in a useful direction?**

8

Patterns & Strategies

"Excellence is a game of inches. It is a thousand things, a thousand, thousand things each done a tiny bit better"

Tom Peters

MODELLING THE PATTERN

We create behavioural habits or patterns in order to achieve certain tasks or to free ourselves up in order to pay attention to other things. All patterns are helpful at the moment of creation; they represent the best choice we have at the time. Usually our patterns are generative and continue as useful to our life, and sometimes our patterns of behaviour are out of date and are no longer helpful.

- Notice what you are doing when things go well and do more of that.
- Pay attention to the unhelpful repetitive patterns you are caught up in and consider changing them.

Modelling the Pattern

One way to assist your client to discover more about how they have constructed their model of the world is by asking them to identify and draw out four components of their specific pattern. Exploring the context, behaviour, trigger and positive intention of the pattern in this way helps your client to appreciate:

- You are clearly interested in their model of the world
- Their pattern operates in certain contexts of their work/life, not all of them
- Their pattern behaviours are different from the intention behind the behaviours
- Their pattern has certain triggers
- They are not their pattern

When dealing with problem patterns the coach can pace the client's unconscious mind by suggesting that they hold-on to the pattern for only as long as the current behaviour is the best choice available to satisfy the positive intention. The coach can also use the model to set a direction in coaching to find the source of the pattern rather than the reason it is there. Metaphorically, if we discover the location of the particular switch on the wall we can turn it off or plug in something else. We do not need to understand electricity to change the way we use it.

As the coaching conversation progresses, the attentive coach can also listen out for:

- The representational system the client is using
- The meta programs that the client uses to filter information
- Assumptions and limiting beliefs that may be maintaining the pattern
- The driving values that support the current pattern and will support future outcomes

This further information allows the coach to formulate an effective and elegant plan for adding resources that will take the client from where they are to where they want to be.

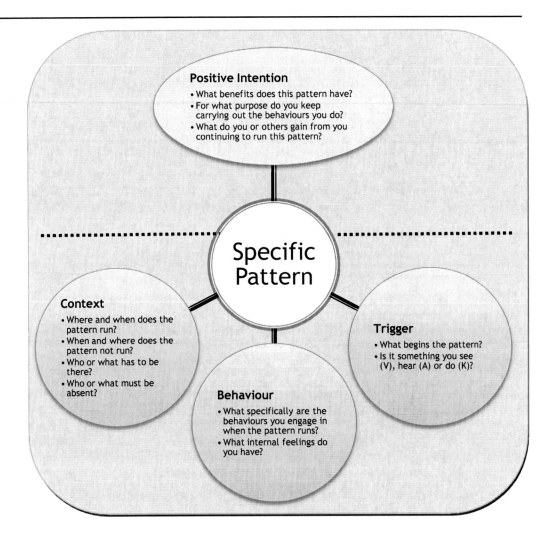

Positive Intention
- What benefits does this pattern have?
- For what purpose do you keep carrying out the behaviours you do?
- What do you or others gain from you continuing to run this pattern?

Specific Pattern

Context
- Where and when does the pattern run?
- When and where does the pattern not run?
- Who or what has to be there?
- Who or what must be absent?

Trigger
- What begins the pattern?
- Is it something you see (V), hear (A) or do (K)?

Behaviour
- What specifically are the behaviours you engage in when the pattern runs?
- What internal feelings do you have?

Constructing the model in this way makes several options for change immediately available for the client to explore:

1. Avoid the trigger
2. Link (anchor) a new response to the trigger
3. Avoid the context
4. Build new skills and resources to cope in the specific context
5. Choose new behaviours that satisfy the positive intention at least as well, or even better than the old behaviour

CHANGING PATTERNS

People have defined insanity as doing the same thing over and over again and expecting different results. In his book "Do One Thing Different" Bill O'Hanlon suggest many ways you can raise awareness and make changes to the unhelpful patterns a person may have in life. Breaking the problem pattern or finding and using solution patterns can be ways to help add new resources to the situation and get different results.

Breaking Problem Patterns
Do Something Different

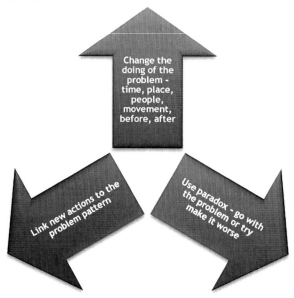

For example:
How I can control my quick breathing and tight chest when waiting to speak out in a group or at a meeting?

Do something different

- **Change the doing of the problem** – change when you speak, where you meet, and the first words you say...
- **Go with the problem or try to make it worse** - accept that's how it is and start quickening your breathing and tightening your chest ahead of time so you are totally prepared for what usually happens
- **Link new actions to the problem pattern** - consciously have a sip of water every time you notice your quick breathing or your chest being tight

Find and Use Solution Patterns
Do More of What Works

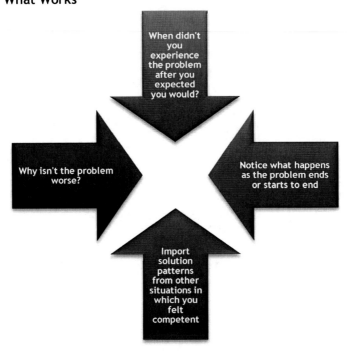

Continuing with the example:
How I can control my quick breathing and tight chest when waiting to speak out in a group or at a meeting?

Do more of what works

- **When didn't you experience the problem after you expected you would?** What was different in you when that happened? How did you do that?
- **Notice what happens as the problem ends or starts to end.** Can you do more of that sooner?
- **Import solution patterns from other situations in which you felt competent.** Have you been confident talking to a group at a party or family gathering? How do you do that?
- **Why isn't the problem worse?** What do you do to maintain the problem and not make it so that you can't speak a single word to anyone and you faint as soon as you open your mouth?

STRATEGIES OF EXCELLENCE

Strategies are the essence of how we go through life. They are the precise thinking processes we use that lead to a specific outcome. A strategy is made up of a sequence of internal representations – pictures, sounds, feelings, self talk, smells and tastes. The precise sequence of what you are paying attention to and how you do it makes the strategy unique.

Most strategies are unconscious and outside of conscious awareness, this makes them automatic and speeds up processing. Each person has a wide selection of many strategies, some larger and some smaller. Some performance related strategies that can form the basis for coaching conversations:

- How do you get in a particular state?
- How do you keep in a particular state?
- How do you know when to start?
- How do you know to carry on?
- How do you know when to stop?
- How do you know you are performing as you want?
- How do you know to change what you are doing?
- How do you recover from mistakes?
- How do you deal with the unknown?
- How do you choose or make decisions?

Discovering Strategies

A strategy has 4 stages. The simplest strategy has four steps and the most complex can have as many as necessary. Usually the more streamlined the strategy the easier it will be for the person to get the outcome they want. By discovering the strategy someone uses when they are "probleming" often the very nature of bringing it into consciousness will begin to give the person choice over their response in the future, they may realise that it is possible to change, should they wish to.

By bringing a strategy to conscious awareness, you can:

- Explore a successful strategy so you can consciously repeat it
- Discover a person's successful strategy so you can use it yourself
- Explore an unsuccessful strategy so you can identify potential areas for change
- Explore a successful strategy in one context so you can use it in another context
- Compare a successful strategy with an unsuccessful strategy so you can discover the difference that makes the difference

The **Trigger**

- What is it that sets the strategy into operation. Is it something you see, something you hear, something you touch, something you smell or something you taste?
- The trigger begins the sequence that leads to getting your outcome.

The **Decision Point - Exit**

- What is the final check that you have got the outcome you wanted - does it make sense, look right, feel right, taste right, sound right or smell right?
- Once the decision has been made the particular strategy exits and you go on to another strategy.

The **Operation** Phase

- What is the sequence of actions you carry out to get your outcome?
- Do you make a picture, talk to yourself, observe, listen, feel a certain way, etc.
- What order do you do those things in?
- What are the critical elements?

feedback

The **Comparison Test**

- How do you know whether you have moved any nearer to your outcome - what is your evidence criteria?
- The test compares where you are now with where you want to be.
- If they match you move on to the final check, the decision point. If they don't match, return to operation phase.

Feedback

Feedback is an essential element of this model. It recognises that when the comparison test reveals you are not getting the results you intended you return to the operation phase. At this point learning from the feedback and having the flexibility to change behaviour is what will help a person achieve their desired outcome.

> *If you always do what you have always done - you'll always get what you have always got*

If a person doesn't have clear evidence criteria for the comparison test, recognise the feedback, or learn whatever they need to learn from it then they are likely to continue in the operation phase indefinitely repeating the same behavioural patterns.

IDENTIFYING A STRATEGY

Eliciting and modifying strategies is a core skill for highly effective NLP practitioners and coaches. In coaching performance it is helpful to modify unhelpful strategies and streamline effective strategies. **Be specific about what you are going to elicit the strategy for.** You may only need to elicit the stages of a strategy that help the person or group towards their outcome. You could:

Discover what starts a strategy
- Identify the trigger for a **performance state** so that you can effectively repeat it at will
- Identify the trigger for an **unwanted state** so that you can effectively collapse the anchor, or link something more resourceful to the trigger

Discover the sequence of operations within the strategy
- Find the sequence of operations a person uses to **solve problems** in one context so they can repeat it in a different context
- **Compare the sequence** of operations a person uses when they do something well and do something badly and discover the difference

Discover how a person is convinced they have what they wanted
- Discover how a person **knows when they have learned** something so you can help them be convinced they have learned about themselves during the coaching
- Discover how a person **knows that they can perform a specific task** and build that into the effects stage of the coaching

Strategy Elicitation Process

1. *Decide on the precise strategy to elicit*

2. *Get the person in the state connected with performing the strategy*
   - Have your client remember a time in rich sensory detail or actually perform the task there and then.

3. *Discover the trigger*
   - How do you know when to start the strategy?
   - Is it something you see, something you hear or something you touch or do?
   - What lets you know it's time to _____?

4. *Discover the operations phase*
   - What do you do inside your mind?
   - Do you make pictures, talk to yourself or feel a certain way?
   - What order do you do these things in?
   - Is there anything else

5. *Discover the comparison test*
   - How do you tell if you have got what you want?
   - How do you track your progress?
   - How do you evaluate alternatives?

6. *Discover the decision point*
   - How do you know when to stop that strategy?
   - Does it make sense, look right, feel right, taste right, sound right or smell right?

7. *Replay the strategy to the client*
   - Take your client through the strategy step by step and check that it leads to their outcome. Go back and discover more steps if you need to.

8. *Improve the strategy*
   - Could anything be added, changed or removed to make the strategy work even better?

9. *What is the next smallest step to take?*

Motivation Strategies

We all have areas at work or in life where we are naturally motivated. In general, effective motivation strategies include:

- A clear definition of what you want at the right level of detail
- Vc+   A visual representation of completing the task and positive consequences
- Ad+   An internal voice with good tonality using modal operators of possibility
- Ki+   A positive feeling that leads to beginning the task

If you elicit a person's motivation strategy in one context, you can use it in another. When constructing a motivation strategy with someone you can either modify an existing strategy in line the above guidelines, or construct a new strategy.

Constructing a motivation strategy

1. *What exactly do you want to be motivated towards?*

2. *Describe the picture you have of you feeling fully motivated and ready to go?*

3. *What will you say to yourself to get you motivated in the right way for you?*

4. *What is the name of the feeling that lets you know you are totally motivated and ready to start?*

5. *What is the next smallest step to take?*

BUILDING A TOWARDS STRATEGY

This set of questions is a guide to how you can use the SCORE framework and the questions within this book as a flowing sequence to help a person resolve a problem or challenge they are currently facing and move towards a desirable outcome. Perhaps you may not ask all 50 questions as they are, but as a coach you may be surprised to discover how well the process can work if you ask yourself the questions and reflect on or write down your answers.

Situation

Describe the situation and symptoms

1.	Where and when do you experience the problem?
2.	What are you seeing, hearing, feeling and doing?
3.	What exactly is the problem for you?
4.	Do you want to make a change?
5.	Do you believe that change is possible and you are capable of doing it?

Cause

Explore the cause using some reversal questions

6.	What do you need to keep on doing in order to maintain this problem?
7.	What beliefs do you have to hold for this problem to persist?
8.	What everything has to be there for this problem to occur?
9.	What would you need to do to make this problem worse?
10.	How do you know when you are about to have this problem?
11.	How can you teach someone else to have to this problem?
12.	Teach me now... what must I do, think, believe and value?
13.	What kind of person do I have to be to have this problem as well?
14.	In order to create this problem in a different context what would you need to do?

15.	What do you do differently in those contexts where you don't have the problem?
16.	There are some people who don't have this problem. What are they doing that is different from what you do?
17.	What do they never do that you sometimes (or often) do?
18.	What advice could you give them from your own personal experience that would help them to create this problem?

Outcome

Define the outcome using proactive language

19.	What do really you want? (ensure the answer is a towards statement)

Check the ecology of the outcome
(and use the confusion state to set up the next section)

20.	What will happen if you get it?
21.	What won't happen if you get it?
22.	What will happen if you don't get it?
23.	What won't happen if you don't get it?
24.	How has not making a change yet not helped you change?

Make the desired outcome well formed

25.	What specifically do you want? (remind me)
26.	How will you know when you have it (see, hear, feel, do)?
27.	Is it in your control?
28.	When, where and with whom?
29.	How will this outcome affect you and others?

Resources

Connect to useful resources

30.	What options do you have?
31.	What beliefs will help you achieve your outcome?
32.	What skills, abilities and support have you got (or can get)?
33.	What would you do if you were a superhero/your team/your boss?
34.	How have you gotten over a challenge like this before?
35.	If a bit of magic happened, what would that be?

Build a motivation strategy

36.	Describe the picture you have of you achieving your goal, feeling fully motivated and ready to go?
37.	Adjust the qualities of the image and sounds to make it even more compelling and desirable.
38.	What will you say to yourself to get you motivated in the right way for you?
39.	What is the name of the feeling that lets you know you are ready to take action?

Integrate conscious and unconscious resources

40.	Tell a story or series of short stories or analogies that pace the experience for your client through five stages - Situation, Cause, Outcome, Resources, Effects

Effects

Consider the effects of achieving the outcome

41.	How will reaching your next goal(s) change things?
42.	What will the impact be on you/your team/your organisation?
43.	How will applying your resources effect the past situation?
44.	What will happen differently in the future?
45.	What is the ultimate benefit of achieving your goal?

Future pace to a time beyond achieving the outcome

46.	Really help the person associate into a future time and look back on when they had the old problem
47.	What solutions do you now have available?

Take action

48.	What is the next smallest step you could take this week?
49.	When will you do it?
50.	How committed are you to taking the next step?

VISUALISING SUCCESS

Visualising or mental imagery works because the mind cannot differentiate between what is real and what is vividly imagined.

In "The Intention Experiment" Lynne McTaggart describes how electromyography with a group of skiers discovered that when they mentally rehearsed their downhill runs, the electrical impulses sent to the muscles were the same as when physically engaged in the runs.

If you imagine yourself going through an event in real time and experience all the sights, sounds and feelings associated you strengthen the neural pathways in the same way as actually performing the activity.

> "I can see the start, the strokes, the walls, the turns, the finish, the strategy, all of it. I can vividly see incredible detail, down even to the wake behind me ... it's like programming a race in my head, and that programming sometimes seems to make it happen just as I had imagined it."
>
> Michael Phelps
> 8 Gold Medals
> Beijing Olympics 2008

Five Steps for Successful Visualisation

Visualisation works best when you break the activity down into stages so that the part of the brain that assists in planning a route to achievement, will not be overwhelmed with too much data.

1. *Decide on the purpose of your visualisation - be specific and make it small*

2. *Mentally warm up by creating the relaxation response*
   Find a quiet place. Get comfortable. Become aware of your breathing and focus on the out breath. Adopt a passive attitude and allow any thoughts that come to mind to pass by.

3. *Use real time images with all the senses*
   Create a movie in your mind. Be as realistic as possible. See what you'd see, hear what you'd hear and feel what you'd feel. Run the movie through seeing yourself perform in the way you want to perform.

4. *Set yourself short sessions*
   Carry out several short sessions regularly throughout the week. If you are losing concentration, stop. Remember what you practice in your mind is most likely to happen in reality.

5. *Practice regularly*
   Everyone is different. Find the best time of day, best place, and best length of time for you. Practice focussing on your inner world and visualising in difficult conditions. Remember practice makes permanent.

Using Visualisation

Visualisation can be used in many ways, including:

- You can help the client visualise themselves performing in the way they want to and anchor it (future pacing).
- You can help a client visualise themselves being the way they want to be and play out several possible scenarios in their mind to check the ecology of a change.
- A client can visualise a certain situation and can visualise what it would be like if they approached the situation in a variety of particular emotional states to build awareness of choice.
- You can ask your client visualise performing a specific action or being in a certain state between sessions.
- You can visualise elements of your performance as a coach.

Some possible uses of visualisation in the context of competition are:

Visualisation	Example
Mental practice of specific skills	Imagining using a specific tool or technique
Controlling arousal and anxiety	Imagining relaxing images to calm nerves
Performance review and analysis	Reviewing a practice session for strong and weak points
Within pre-event routines	Imagining focussing in the 10 minutes before an event starts
Improving confidence and positive thinking	Imagining previous successful performances
Preparation for an event	Imagining performing well in different conditions – noise, quiet, distractions, luck, officials, etc.
Tactical rehearsal	Imagining reading a project brief and planning your approach and timings
Maintaining mental freshness	Imagining your end of event day routine

THE NEW BEHAVIOUR GENERATOR

This technique can help you create a visualisation to master/improve an existing behaviour or gain a new one. It is a sophisticated approach to changing behaviour and is adapted from Transformations by Bandler and Grinder. For the new behaviours to occur easily and naturally, they should be as effective as or even more effective than the old behaviour and meet the same higher intention.

For example to improve an old behaviour of an average serve in tennis, the new behaviour of an outstanding serve would need to be compatible with their higher intention of, say, a friendly game of mixed doubles. If the new behaviour was selected without reference to the higher intention then the new behaviour is unlikely to occur in the desired way in the desired context.

Improving Performance

1. *Identify the behaviour you want to improve*

2. *Create a movie and watch and listen to yourself performing the current behaviour 'out in front of yourself'*

3. *Think about what new behaviour or response you would prefer to make in the situation*

4. *Watch and listen to yourself as you make that new response in the situation*

5. *Repeat several times, each time noticing the fine distinctions in sight, sound, feeling, touch, taste and smell.*

6. *Ask yourself are there any more adjustments you need to make?*

7. *Repeat with any fine adjustments made.*

8. *Run the movie now from the perspective of being there and having all the feelings that go along with that particular response. Enjoy the positive feelings.*

9. *Ask your mind to take responsibility for having this new behaviour naturally occur in the situation where the old behaviour used to.*

Modelling the Behaviour or Skill of Someone Else

1. Identify the behaviour you want to have or to master.

2. Create a movie and watch and listen to yourself performing the current behaviour 'out in front of yourself'

3. Select a person who performs in that kind of situation in a way that you thing is quite appropriate, elegant and effective and a way in which you would like to.

4. Close your eyes and watch your model carefully exhibiting the excellence or doing the behaviour you would like to have. Notice the fine distinctions in sight, sound, feeling, touch, taste and smell to get a strong, clear representation of them doing it.

5. Play the movie again with you alongside your exemplar, doing exactly what they do, saying what they say, seeing what they see

6. Now watch and listen to yourself as you perform this behaviour in a new way

7. Ask yourself are there any more adjustments you need to make?

8. Repeat with any fine adjustments made.

9. Run the movie now from the perspective of being there and having all the feelings that go along with that particular response. Enjoy the positive feelings.

10. Ask your mind to take responsibility for having this new behaviour naturally occur in the situation where the old behaviour used to.

DISNEY CREATIVITY STRATEGY

Robert Dilts was fascinated by the idea of creativity and applied NLP to model several recognised geniuses and discover more about how they got the results they did. One of the people he modelled was Walt Disney, someone who built a very successful organisation fundamentally based on creativity.

The modelling process revealed three distinct roles that Disney played, each involving a particular type of thinking and action:

- The Dreamer - the visionary who dreamt up ideas for films and business ventures where anything was possible.
- The Realist - the pragmatic producer who made things happen.
- The Critic - the eagle-eyed evaluator who refined what the Dreamer and Realist produced so that it appealed to the audience.

> "Creativity as a total process involves the coordination of these three sub-processes: dreamer, realist and critic. A dreamer without a realist cannot turn ideas into tangible expressions. A critic and a dreamer without a realist just become stuck in a perpetual conflict. The dreamer and a realist might create things, but they might not achieve a high degree of quality without a critic. The critic helps to evaluate and refined the products of creativity."
>
> Robert B. Dilts
> *Strategies of Genius: Volume 1*

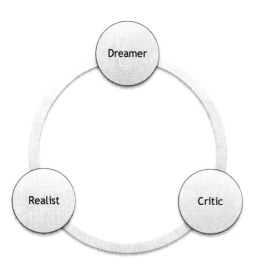

The creative strategy process uses these three particular roles and is very useful in coaching with individuals and groups for establishing a team vision, planning for the future or exploring a chosen goal.

- Which role(s) do you feel most comfortable with?
- Which role(s) do you find most challenging?
- Which role(s) could you develop even more?

Disney's Creative Cycle

1. *Establish a neutral position and select 3 distinct physical locations – dreamer, realist and critic.*

2. *For each space elicit and anchor the appropriate state and physiology.*
   - **Dreamer** *"a time when you could dream or fantasise freely"*. Physiology: Head and eyes up. Posture symmetrical and relaxed.
   - **Realist** *"a time when you could plan realistically, put ideas into action"*. Physiology: Head and eyes straight ahead or slightly forward. Posture symmetrical and slightly forward.
   - **Critic** *"a time when you could constructively criticise, as well as notice problems"*. Physiology: Eyes down. Head down and tilted. Posture angular.

3. *Pick a specific outcome to explore.*

4. *Step into the Dreamer location and start to imagine the outcome you would like.*
   - Allow yourself to "go for it" and think in an open and uninhibited way.
   - *"What is possible, what could we do?" "What would the benefit be?"*

5. *Step in the Realist space and take the dream and feel yourself in the positions of all the relevant characters.*
   - Consider a possible sequence of activities that will lead to achieving the outcome.
   - *"How can we practically implement the ideas?" "What specifically are the steps to take?"*

6. *Step in the Critic space and find out what is missing or needed. Turn criticisms into "how" questions.*
   - It is often helpful to have the critic acknowledge the satisfactory elements so far and only criticise the plan, not the Realist or the Dreamer.
   - *"Why might someone object to the idea?" "Who will be affected by the new idea?"*

7. *Step into a neutral position and consider all that you have learned so far.*
   - When you have a clear idea of what else there is to discover return to the Dreamer position and repeat Steps 4 to 6 as until your plan congruently fits each position.

8. *What is your next step that will take you in a useful direction?*

9

Metaphors
and Stories

"And God said 'let there be light' and there was light,
but the Electricity Board said he would have to wait
until Thursday to be connected"

Spike Milligan

THE METAPHORS WE LIVE BY

We describe the world in many and varied ways and it is essential to remember that *"the map is not the territory."* There may be a reality (really real, happening, absolutely) and there are descriptions of reality (words, symbols, pictures, music, movement, anything that we make and do).

Generally, a metaphor is defined as a way of speaking in which one thing is expressed in terms of another, whereby this bringing together throws new light on the character of what is being described. In NLP we use the term metaphor to encompass stories, analogies, and similes – in fact anything where we are likening one thing to another, whether directly or indirectly.

> *"Metaphor is for most people a device of the poetic imagination and the rhetorical flourish... most people think they can get along perfectly well without metaphor. We have found, on the contrary, that metaphor is pervasive in everyday life, not just in language but in thought and action"*
>
> *Lakoff & Johnson*
> Metaphors We Live By

Every word is a metaphor

You can't get a real cat in through your ears, no more than I can make one come out of my mouth. The word "cat" is a metaphor for an existing creature that lives, breathes and scratches.

Metaphors at Work

Some people see the world as a jungle fraught with dangers they have to fight through. They say things like *"It's a jungle out there!"* Some see life as a race, and it is important to win. They say things like *"We're on the last leg now"* or *"My Dad's handed me the batten."* Some see their business as a family or an army or an obstacle course. Some see their family as a test or a competition or even a tool box.

The metaphors we use to define our experiences shape and influence our life. They create neurological links and associations that drive our internal representations, states and behaviours. Ask yourself:

- If you had to describe your work at the moment as a book, TV series, play or film would it be a comedy, tragedy, black comedy, thriller or farce? What would be the title?
- What metaphors do you have for relationships?
- What are you metaphors for health?

Metaphorical Coaching

Be creative and explore your client's metaphor using the SCORE model as a framework to guide your conversation.

1. *Do you have a situation or topic you are willing to explore metaphorically?*

2. *Ask your client to describe their current situation* (very briefly)

3. *And if you were to think about the situation metaphorically, when _____, what is that like for you?*

4. *If your current situation is like _____* (calibrate to an unconscious yes), *then...*
   This part seems to work equally well when run almost content free - the coach directs the process and the client consider their answers to themselves. Expand on each of the stages below to help your client explore their metaphor. If necessary remind the client the metaphor is like a story and anything can happen in a story.

   - *Situation*
       - *How is the metaphor playing out at the moment?*
       - *What is going well, what is not going so well?*

   - *Cause*
       - *Who are the main characters, what are they doing?*
       - *What is the intention behind their actions?*

   - *Outcome*
       - *What would be the best next stage in the story?*

   - *Resources*
       - *What skills, abilities or behaviours allow the story to play out successfully?*
       - *What support is needed, and where does it come from?*

   - *Effect*
       - *What happens as the story unfolds?*
       - *How do all parts in the story benefit in the end?*

5. *What is different now, what has changed for you?*

6. *What is your next step that will take you in a useful direction?*

USING METAPHORS FOR A CHANGE

Metaphor is behind the NLP presupposition we already have all the resources we need, or can create them. A metaphor is like salt and pepper – too much may spoil the taste but a little sprinkled on your food will bring out the flavour.

Metaphors for Creating States

You can use a small story of an everyday experience to encourage the listener to change their current state and connect with a more useful state. For example after listening to your client explain the situation and the cause of their problem you might tell a short story about the choices you have in selecting which film to go and see at the weekend. After you have elicited a decision making state, you may then ask your client an outcome question like *"what do you want to have happen?"*

To come up with a metaphor for creating states ask yourself:

- What is the emotional state I am trying to convey and what is an example of that in everyday life?

To elicit the state of curiosity you could tell a story like: *"I was putting on a coat I hadn't worn for a while when I reached into the pocket and touched something unexpected yet familiar. Immediately, my fingers jumped away but they found themselves drawn back to discover more. This time they delved further than before and I discovered something very useful..."* Stopping the story at this point will probably leave you listeners searching for the answer to what you discovered in your pocket. You could allow them to come up with their own answer or finish the story: *"I recognised I had found some change and began to think about how much it was and how I was going to use it in the future"*

Metaphors for a Change

A metaphor invites the imagination to explore associations and meaning at an unconscious level. With an isomorphic metaphor the structure of the metaphor matches the structure of the clients situation and the metaphor includes within it information to help the client resolve or improve their situation. This complex form of metaphor is a very effective technique in coaching change.

> *"Metaphors, in the form of fairytales, parables, and anecdotes, are consciously and unconsciously used by therapists in order to assist a client in making the changes he wants to make"*
>
> *David Gordon*
> Therapeutic Metaphors

The art of constructing isomorphic metaphor is covered fully in David Gordon's excellent book 'Therapeutic Metaphors'.

Metaphors for Instructions

Analogies or similes (where one thing is likened to another) are particularly effective where there is a need for speed such as in business and with teenagers. The metaphor conveys more than just the facts; it contains some of the helpful beliefs, values and actions that support learning or understanding. By making a comparison using AS or LIKE, we can open up links for the listener to expand their understanding.

- What is the skill I am trying to convey and what is that like in everyday life?

For instance learning to tie a knot for climbing or sailing can be likened to learning to tie your shoelaces – you have to get the ends equal and the knot neat. There was a time when we all had to concentrate to tie our shoelaces but now can pretty much tie a perfect knot without thinking about it. Similarly, learning can be like planting flowers - a seed is planted in my mind which I nurture with water and sun to help it grow.

- What are your metaphors for learning?
- What are your metaphors for coaching?

Adding Metaphorical Resources

Metaphorical resources allow the listener to bridge the gap between their current situation and their desired outcome. Some possible resources to include in your story are:

- Communicating in a different representational system (VAK)
- An empowering belief (I can achieve whatever I put my mind to)
- A resourceful state (confident, relaxed, energised, focussed, curious…)
- A chain of states (hesitation-frustration-impatience-desire-action)
- A specific strategy (Vc+, Ad+, Ki+)
- Specific knowledge or behaviour (first step, saying hello, making a phone call…)

A character in your story can use the resources to resolve their situation or can deliver the resource as a direct message, for example *"I'm not sure how to respond to you right now, but I'm sure that if my grandfather was here he'd look you straight in the eye and say___"*

Your Personal Metaphor and Story Bank

By listening, practicing and revising your metaphors you can create a bank of stories that you can use to assist clients when coaching. Whether the source of your metaphor is your own experience, a friends experience, a book or the internet you should always be prepared to adjust the story and deliver it in a way that matches your listener's situation and assists them towards their outcome.

METAPHORICAL STORYTELLING

A metaphorical story can engage the conscious mind fully and allow the listeners unconscious mind to get straight to work making useful links and associations. Metaphor takes the listener beyond one meaning to many possible meanings.

Telling your story

Storytelling is magic in part because it's *personal*. Each day we have new and unique experiences that create our own natural library of stories to share. If you tell stories based on your own experience they can be easier to remember and you can easily access the emotional states in the story that bring it to life. Change names if you need to or just be general, a person I know was once...

Consider the point of your story

Is it a story about the forest or the trees? Or is it about the landscape the trees are in? Or is it about the creatures that live in the forest? A great story is short and to the point. A shallow metaphor is ideal in a business context and is one in which your client may be aware of the correlation between the story and their situation. A deep metaphor is where your listener's conscious mind is not able to track the point of the story and their unconscious mind is invited to create the associations themselves and find their own unique meaning from the story - ideal for personal growth.

Six Tips for storytelling

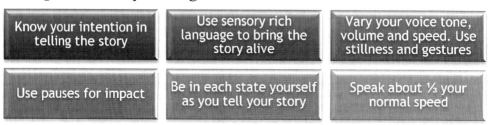

Know your intention in telling the story	Use sensory rich language to bring the story alive	Vary your voice tone, volume and speed. Use stillness and gestures
Use pauses for impact	Be in each state yourself as you tell your story	Speak about ⅓ your normal speed

Creating Stories for a Change

Using the SCORE model is a very effective way to structure a whole story. You can use the 5 phases of the model to tell a flowing story that is either a shallow or deep metaphor.

For example: *"I once heard of a company faced with the challenge of falling sales caused by a global economic downturn that wanted to keep all their staff employed. The secret turned out to be closer to home than they thought. Instead of keeping everything hidden from their staff, they discovered that by engaging people in all parts of the business they had access to a wealth of creativity and talent that not only helped them solve the current problem, it helped shape a long term stable future for the company."*

Natural World Stories and Metaphors

The natural world is full of opportunities for constructing metaphorical stories: Water always finds the most efficient way to flow around obstacles or carrying them along and depositing them somewhere else; Snakes shed their skin; The tides ebb and flow, carry ships and yachts, and bring waves that crash to the shore that surfers play in; Seeds are carried by the wind and other methods to land, some in rich soil and some in barren land but once they receive light, warmth and water they have within themselves all they need to begin growing; Birds find themselves inside an egg, break out, grow feathers and wings and take flight. Using 2nd position is a good way to create a metaphorical story.

Situation	• High in the treetops, overlooking the woodland a bird found itself in its' nest one day. Bird was feeling a little bored and was wondering how they came to be in this situation. Bird generally did a lot of thinking, a lot of waiting and not much doing.
Cause	• Today, there were less siblings in the nest than yesterday. Birds parents were away as usual and some of Birds brothers and sisters had already made their first flight. Bird had not yet discovered how to trust and know what to do for the best.
Outcome	• A caterpillar arrived on a nearby branch. Caterpillar struck up a conversation before Bird could entertain ideas of eating it. "What's the future got in store for you?" Caterpillar asked. Bird thought long and hard about the answer. It wasn't a question Bird was used to answering.
Resources	• Bird said that the future was full of possibility. Bird asked Caterpillar the same question. Caterpillar replied that it had always known deep down inside what to do next. Caterpillar was about to build it's cocoon and shed it's old skin. Caterpillar had been looking forward to this moment since the morning.
Effect	• Bird was still curious. "What happens then?" Bird asked. Caterpillar said that she was destined to be a beautiful butterfly and would fly wherever the wind took her enjoying every moment. Bird got a warm and pleasant feeling deep inside and started testing its wings...

CONSTRUCTING STORIES

When constructing stories use sensory language to bring experiences to life and balance detail and artful vagueness to keep the story interesting. Including patterns from the Milton Model is a very effective way of constructing stories that direct the listener's attention to their own experiences.

- Where it matters to defining the process, relationship or character then give the details in full.
- Where precise content is not essential then allow the listener to fill the details in for themselves.

Five ways to introduce and link stories
1. Once upon a time there was _____
2. My friend John had a particular problem and asked me what to do about it, so I told him a story about _____
3. Whilst the magician was going about his business, mixing up new potions and practicing miracles, he heard a sound in the background of a storyteller just about to begin. The magician listened in_____
4. George was moving some boxes from the attic and was going to take them to the tip when he saw an interestingly coloured book on the top of the pile. It felt heavy as he picked it up and started to read about_____
5. .... After he had enjoyed reminiscing he had a long think about what was important to keep, and what it was time to let go. He knew that less clutter meant more time to focus on the future, his grandmother had taught him that when he sat on her knee at story time. She would tell wondrous and enchanting tales like _____

Representational system language brings the story to life
If you look to include words from all the representational systems as you speak (visual, auditory, kinaesthetic, olfactory and gustatory), you can help your audience get in touch with your story and taste the adventure and learnings that you want them to sniff out. The real world is full of sensory experience. Good stories are as well.

Link concepts and ideas with transitional words
Transitional words allow you to tell a flowing story that joins two sentences together and leads the listener from one thought to another just as easily as listening to the interesting variations in tone and speed in your speech. For example "*as George realised how much he had achieved so far he knew it meant that future success and a terrific sense of pride were guaranteed because of what he had done.*"

- Mild linkages : and, as, while, when, during, before, after, successively, previously, even as
- Strong linkages : because, makes, causes, requires, means

Be Specifically Vague

Use general terms in the resources phase of the story that encourage the listener to select the best resource for them and their specific situation. For example, instead of saying that *"Mr. James knew that if he planted 4 tomato seeds, one from each variety, in the first week of April it would mean he would have a good harvest later in the year"* consider saying *"the gardener knew what to do to help him get exactly what he wanted."* Four useful patterns from the Milton Model for being specifically vague:

Lack of referential index

Using words that don't convey precisely <u>who</u> and <u>where</u> something is so the listener can select what best fits their experience.

- E.g. It, them, they, people, someone, others, everyone, etc

The green dragons best friend, George was lurking under the bed in the 2nd floor room that overlooked the gardens.	<u>Someone</u> was lurking <u>somewhere</u> in the castle.

Unspecified verbs

Deliberately not defining <u>how</u> a particular action was carried out allows the listener to choose the exact manner that fits for them.

- E.g. Helped, leant, felt, understood, knew, went, etc.

George crept towards the wardrobe and opened the door slowly before jumping in feet first and squealing with delight.	George <u>went</u> into the wardrobe.

Nominalisations

By freezing a process in time a nominalisation invites the listener to define <u>in what way</u> the event took place.

- E.g. Awareness, understood, relationship, communication, knowledge, etc.

After he jumped George was aware of a growing feeling that he didn't know if he was hiding or going after something.	After the jump came an <u>awareness</u> of his situation.

Embedded commands

Inserting a listener's name into the sentence and/or marking out the words with a specific emphasis can highlight the parts of the sentence you want the listener to give special attention.

And when he came out, this time he left it all behind.	*And when he came out, this time, _____, HE LEFT IT ALL BEHIND.*

10

Positive Coaching

"We can easily forgive a child who is afraid of the dark; the real tragedy of life is when men are afraid of the light"

Plato

POSITIVE COACHING

The flow of life is unique and special to each of us. In all areas of work and life, our experience is a constant series of events one after another that sometimes happen by design, and sometimes seem to happen without planning. Whether we intend to or not we are always working towards a goal of some sort.

> *"Our plans miscarry because they have no aim. When a man does not know what harbour he is making for, no wind is the right wind"*
>
> *Seneca*

NLP assumes human behaviour is naturally goal orientated. Rather than focus on what is wrong and how it happened, NLP is concerned with the desired outcome or result. Being solution focussed in your coaching and creating congruent "well-formed outcomes" helps people think about the result they truly want and how best can this be achieved.

- Always establish a clear outcome or goal in your coaching
- Our outcomes direct our perceptions and influence our actions

Positive Outcomes

When you ask the question *"What do you want?"* make sure the answer is specific and stated in the positive, i.e. towards what the person wants and not away-from what they don't want.

For example, when your client says *"I don't want to mess up again"* or *"I want to get better at work"*, pace their answer and ask them for a positive outcome: *"I realise that you don't want to mess up again and you want to get better at work, what specifically is it that you do want?"* Sometimes your client will answer right away, sometimes it may take a number of questions before they reveal their outcome *"I want to deliver sales presentations with confidence."* From this starting point you can then ensure their chosen outcome is "well formed" before identifying any additional resources they need.

Helping your client be clear about what they want will create a mental set to move them closer to their goal. When a person has a positive representation of what they want they can be open to noticing new opportunities. It works in the same way as when you find yourself spotting certain makes or colours of car just after you or a close friend has changed their car.

Systemic Focus

We operate as part of a system at work, in our life and within ourselves. There are multiple causes for every situation and multiple consequences when changes are made. We are each a part of an interconnected and interdependent system and no matter what we are doing at any one time results are guaranteed.

- Work towards ecological and desirable consequences as you coach.

Clean Outcomes

Clean Language is a way of asking questions that aims to stay as fully as possible in the persons model of the world. It was modelled by James Lawley and Penny Tompkins from the work of David Grove, who used it in order to introduce as few of his own assumptions and metaphors as possible and give the client maximum freedom for their own thinking.

Using clean language can be a very effective way of helping a person exploring the meaning behind what they say. The following process for beginning a coaching session works best if you follow the script exactly.

1. *For this session to work for you, it needs to be like what?*
   Answer X
   - *And what kind of X is that X*
   - *And is there anything else about that X*

2. *And for this session to be like X, you need to be like what?*
   Answer Y
   - *And what kind of Y is that Y*
   - *And is there anything else about that Y*

3. *And for you to be like Y, I need to be like what?*
   Answer Z
   - *And what kind of Z is that Z*
   - *And is there anything else about that Z*

The two bullet point questions above are very useful to discover more about what your clients means when they identify a state (motivation, confidence, calm, etc.) or uses a nominalisation (communication, relationship, teamwork, etc.)

Focussing on the First Step

The Chinese philosopher Lau Tsu is often quoted as saying *"the journey of a thousand miles begins with a single step"*. In fact, it doesn't matter whether your client is setting off on a journey of 1000 miles or to the end of their garden path, each step will take them closer to whatever they are focussing on.

Even big goals began with a simple first step. Learning to drive starts with phone call to book a lesson, passing an exam starts with choosing the course, a wonderful holiday starts with booking the annual leave. When looking back from the place of having achieved a goal the first steps can be easier to spot.

- What was the first step you took to being a great coach?
- What is the next smallest step for you to continue to be a great coach?

EMOTIONAL CHOICE

Broadly speaking emotions are generally considered positive or negative. Both have value in everyday life and, though we may not want to directly cultivate negative emotions, it is important to recognise their benefit in motivating us away from perceived danger. Positive emotions are not only pleasurable to experience, they act as a buffer to the challenges we face at work and in our lives. Positive emotion has been shown to help people solve problems and be more creative.

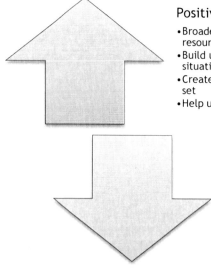

Positive Emotions

- Broaden our intellectual, physical and social resources
- Build up reserves we can draw on in challenging situations.
- Create an expansive, tolerant and creative mental set
- Help us to be open to new ideas and new experience

Negative Emotions

- Are rooted in survival and fight, flight or conserve responses
- Fear, sadness , disgust and anger are our first line of defence against threats
- Motivate us away-from perceived danger

Negative emotions are usually best left in the past. Helping your clients separate historic emotion from current emotions allows them to focus on their here and now experience. Many people are not aware of how their breathing shifts when they feel negative emotions. Bringing this to your clients awareness when coaching and helping them discover and use one breath relaxation can be a very useful intervention. Being comfortable *"feeling the fear and doing it anyway"* can assist people in responding in an appropriate and resourceful ways to any challenges they face.

- By building awareness of emotions you provide space to choose the response

In general positive emotions should be celebrated and actively promoted whenever your client identifies them. They can be further developed by:

- Adopting a growth mindset
- Increasing optimism and hope
- Using your signature strengths as often as possible
- Connecting to your inner happiness and joy
- Showing gratitude to your support team

Emotional Waiting

Sometimes people confuse their goals with their desired emotions, for example they'll say *"I want to be confident"* and then put steps in place that must be achieved before they can feel confident. This works fine if they achieve the steps along the way, but all too often things change, a key step is missed out and the person never feels the desired emotion. They end up spending all their time waiting to experience the emotion, but never getting round to feeling it.

A common example is people who say *"I'll be _____ when_____"*. For example: *"I'll be happy when I have a relationship"* or *"I'll be motivated when they give me a pay rise."*

Sometimes the very thing a person is putting off, is just what they need to get what they want. If a person is motivated at work they are much more likely to get a pay rise; if they are happy within themselves they are being the sort of person with which someone else would like to begin a relationship.

- Emotional freedom is choosing your here and now experience.
- Recognise your emotional state and change it when you need to

Emotional Flexibility

This process is a very effective way to prepare for a challenge ahead by selecting the most appropriate emotional state for the situation.

1. *Identify a situation in which you'd like to explore your emotional response.*

2. *Imagine yourself in that situation, clearly and in detail. Make a mini movie of your mind's eye. What do you see, what do you hear?*

3. *When you have firmly established the movie, select an emotion. Imagine feeling that emotion in that situation and discover your possible response.*

   - If I feel ____(emotion)____ in this situation, what will be the consequences?

4. *When you have thoroughly explored your reaction, select another emotion and imagine feeling it in the same context. Notice how your reaction and response in the situation changes when you feel the new emotion.*

5. *Keeping the situation constant, run through 5 or 6 different emotions observing the variations in your response.*

   - Use a variety of diverse emotions to explore the possible consequences. For example excited, anxious, sad, confident, aroused, lazy, focused, joyful, etc.

6. *What would be the most resourceful emotion to choose if you meet that situation in the future?*

GROWTH MINDSET

The way we think about ourselves and our intelligence, our talents and personality shapes our life at work and at home. After over 10 years research on achievement and success Carol Dweck from Stanford University concluded that people can have one of two different mindsets in a certain situation – a fixed mindset or a growth mindset.

> *"People with growth mindset love what they do even when they are faced with challenges"*
>
> *Carol Dweck*

Fixed Mindset	Growth Mindset
•People with a fixed mindset believe that their traits are just givens. They have a certain amount of brains and talent and nothing can change that. They: •Want to look good at all costs •Believe that talent should come naturally •Hide mistakes and conceal deficiencies	•People with a growth mindset see their qualities as things that can be developed through their dedication and effort. They: •Emphasise learning something new over everything else •Believe the harder you work, the better you can become •Capitalise on mistakes and confront their own deficiencies

Mindsets are beliefs about yourself and your most basic qualities. They are often learned from others and naturally reinforced in the way we give and receive praise. Offering praise based purely on the talent that a person appears to possess encourages them to seek chances to reinforce that same behaviour again. They tend to chose tasks which they know they can achieve, so that they can appear 'expert' or 'talented' as often as possible.

When you offer praise based on the process, or effort, that the person has gone through, you encourage them to continue the process of learning. They are less likely to be worried by poor results, as long as they feel they are learning something.

Coaching a Growth Mindset

Coaching with a growth mindset involves asking questions and offering feedback that values passion, effort, strategies and progress. For example:

- How can you develop your skills and abilities in this area even more?
- You've shown determination and perseverance. How did you do it?
- How did you get better at something that you used to be not so good at?
- Think of someone who learned something which you didn't think they would be able to learn. What can you learn from how they achieved it?

Learn more at www.mindsetonline.com or in "Mindset" by Carol Dweck.

OPTIMISM & HOPE

The way we think about and describe the events that happen to us, at work and in our life, are generally accepted to fall in one of two attitudes - optimism or pessimism. As the saying goes *"Is the glass half full or half empty?"* We can recognise optimism and pessimism in the language people use *"I had a great day today, I love my work"* and *"It rained today, that's the end of the summer"*. When some people make a mistake or suffer a setback it seems to be the end of the world *"I'm no good at drawing, I'm not a creative person."* Other people just shrug their shoulders and move on *"I struggled in that meeting but I've learned lots for next time."*

The way a person explains the events that have happened reveals the belief which is influencing their emotional states and behaviours.

Permanent or Temporary

Optimistic people think good events are permanent (I'm always lucky) and bad events are temporary (diets don't work when I eat out). Pessimists think bad events are permanent (diets never work) and good events are temporary (my lucky day).

Universal or Specific

Optimistic people think good events are universal (I'm creative) and bad events are specific (that meeting was unsuccessful). Pessimists think bad events are universal (the project is a failure) and good events are specific (I solved one problem before).

Challenging Pessimism

Challenging any pessimistic thinking your client may be using is a key part of coaching. The patterns in Section 5 for shifting perspectives are useful ways to help someone discover alternatives and dispute the evidence, implications and usefulness of holding a particular belief.

Hope

When people are hopeful for the future they bounce back from a setback in one area of their life and get on a roll easily when they experience success. People who feel hopeless or despairing tend to collapse under pressure across many areas of their life and rarely get on a roll.

	Good things are	Bad things are
Hopeful	Permanent and Universal	Temporary and Specific
Hopeless	Temporary and Specific	Permanent and Universal

Building Optimism and Hope

Practising the patterns an optimist uses is a proven way to increase optimism and hope. Encourage your clients to dispute any pessimistic thoughts and:

- Consider good things as likely to last and generate even more positive events
- Think about bad things as one-offs that they can learn from and move on

FOCUSSING ON STRENGTHS

For as long as I can remember, I have always believed that we have within us a set of strengths and qualities we can draw on. Some of these will be encouraged by parents and teachers whist growing up, and some may lay dormant for years. Rather like the beauty within a spring meadow, all the seeds are there and are ready and willing to come to life under the right conditions.

> "Use your signature strengths every day in the main realms of your life to bring about abundant gratification and authentic happiness."
>
> Martin Seligman PhD
> *(Authentic Happiness)*

If we are going to label ourselves, let it be positive!

In seeking to develop an intellectually rigorous and scientifically grounded classification of strengths Dr. Martin Seligman and Dr. Chris Peterson conducted research over a period of 3 years. They identified 6 virtues common throughout great Eastern and Western religious traditions and modern thinking: Wisdom, Courage, Humanity, Justice, Temperance and Transcendence. The 24 character strengths represent possible routes for a person to achieve those virtues.

- What are you character strengths as a coach?
- How easily do you notice the strengths in others?

Researchers have given character strengths a central role in the field of positive psychology and consider strengths as **the enabler of pleasure, flow, and other positive experiences**. A study of 3907 individuals showed that the 5 character strengths of **hope, zest, gratitude, curiosity,** and **love** show a robust, consistent relationship with life satisfaction (Park, Peterson, & Seligman, 2004).

Signature Strengths

Out of all our strengths, some will represent our true and authentic self, and some are the result of experiences and learning - perhaps those skills that we needed to develop to thrive at home or in our work. Signature Strengths are those that you feel are authentically you and are where at least one of the following will apply:

- You feel "this is the real me"
- They are invigorating to use, not exhausting
- They are exciting to learn and apply
- You feel joy, zest and enthusiasm using them
- They are a part of your personal hobbies and interests
- You have a sense of "try and stop me" when using them

The 24 Character Strengths

Creativity	Curiosity	Judgment and Open-Mindedness
Love of learning	Perspective	Bravery
Perseverance	Honesty	Zest
Capacity to Love and Be Loved	Kindness	Social Intelligence
Teamwork	Fairness	Leadership
Forgiveness and mercy	Modesty and Humility	Prudence
Self-Regulation	Appreciation of Beauty and Excellence	Gratitude
Hope	Humour	Religiousness and Spirituality

(Source: www.viacharacter.org)

Using Character Strengths in Coaching

Focussing on strengths helps a person meet challenges in a positive and resourceful way. There are strong links between using your strengths and a person's level of happiness and their performance at work. Some options for using strengths:

- Celebrate your top 5 signature strengths
- Use your signature strengths as frequently and in as many settings as you can
- Build your life and work around your strengths
- Remember where you have used a strength in the past, and plan how you can use it even more in both new opportunities and tough challenges.
- Identify and develop the strengths that will help you achieve your goals
- Use your less well developed strengths more often. Who can support you to do this?

Discovering Strengths

Providing clear feedback as a coach can help your clients recognise the strengths they have and use. Two options for assessing strengths are:

Take a free online survey

The easiest and most comprehensive way to assess your strengths is to complete the VIA Inventory of Strengths online at www.viacharacter.org The 240-item questionnaire is free and takes approximately 30 minutes to complete. It gives you an immediate report showing your 5 top strengths and a description of each strength.

Self assessment

Simply read through the above list and identify what you consider your signature strengths – those you get a positive energy from using. Rank your strengths in order to create your top 5. You can also read the descriptions for each strength and complete a self assessment in Authentic Happiness by Martin Seligman.

A Strengths Based Coaching Conversation

1. *Tell me about a recent experience where you were really "in your element" at work or in your life and you felt like you were your authentic self.*

2. *What strengths were you using at the time?*
   You can also give your client feedback: *"as you were describing the situation it seemed to me you were using the strengths of _____ and _____"*

3. *How could you use those strengths in a new way in the coming week?*

4. *What would you need, if anything, to make that possible?*

5. *What will the ultimate benefit be if you use your strengths in more situations, more often?*

PLAYING TO YOUR STRENGTHS

This process helps you reflect on when you have been your true self and focus on being more of the real you and using your strengths in order to meet and overcome a current challenge or obstacle in your life.

1. ### Think of 5 experiences in your life when you have felt alive.

   Capture small moments in your life when you were engaged and living / working / playing with a sense of being the real you.

Experience 1	
Experience 2	
Experience 3	
Experience 4	
Experience 5	

2. ### What would an outside observer say were 3 skills, qualities or abilities that you showed at these times?

   Think carefully about what they would compliment you for.

Strength 1	
Strength 2	
Strength 3	

3. ### Think of how you could use these strengths in a new way.

   Stop for a moment and consider a challenge you are currently facing. How would these strengths be a helpful resource for you?

Strength 1	
Strength 2	
Strength 3	

4. ### Identify the next smallest step.

   Which resource can you use in the next few days that will help you meet and overcome the challenge you have been facing?

Next Step	

COACHING HAPPINESS

Happiness is all around us and is one thing that many people would say *"yes please"* to if you offered them more happiness at work, more happiness at home or more happiness in their relationships. It is likely that the desire for more happiness or longer sustained happiness or a return to the happiness they used to have will lie behind many of the goals or outcomes your clients have.

Happiness is a common word with an uncommon meaning

Happiness tends to be one of those emotional states that *"we know it when we feel it."* It can come in a moment of sensory pleasure - the first taste of ice cream on a hot day or the satisfaction and positive emotion of completing a project or being successful. A further level of happiness can be described as the inner joy and contentment of being authentically you.

- The way you define happiness will influence the way you experience happiness

The following tips are drawn from Robert Holden's work and make a very powerful starting point when working with a client who wants to explore more happiness in their life or work.

1. *Define what happiness means to you*
   Happiness is a way of travelling, not a destination. You don't need to search for it out there – just look inside yourself. Choose happiness rather than chase happiness.

2. *Accept your right to be happy – it's your true nature.*
   Let go of the rules you have for happiness, you don't have to work hard or suffer to earn happiness. Life is easier when you start by being kind to yourself.

3. *Find your passion – notice what inspires and delights you.*
   Ask yourself *"When am I at my happiest?"* to discover your real purpose and joy. Do more of what you love.

4. *Enjoy the simple pleasures*
   Laughter, fun and dancing to your favourite music costs nothing yet can be priceless. What would be on your list of simple pleasures?

5. *Develop an attitude of gratitude*
   Think of three things you are grateful for each day and write them down. Do it every day for 2 weeks or more. Giving thanks for the gifts in your life is a proven way to increase your happiness.

6. *Make time for love and friendship*
   Don't be so busy that you neglect your most important relationships at home and at work. Who would you like to spend more time with, be more loving with, and have more fun with?

7. *Practice forgiveness*
   Shift happens when you let go of old grievances or guilt. It releases you from the past and changes your future.

8. *Be present – happiness is where you are, right here, right now.*
   Don't miss out on life by dwelling in the past or striving for a perfect future. Give yourself a present, and savour every moment.

HIGHER PURPOSE

Our higher purpose is revealed in those experiences where we are using our strengths and are fully being our authentic self in the moment. By recognising moments at work or in life when you have been in your element and showed your true spirit, you can look for a common theme that binds the experiences together. Happiness comes when you make choices and decisions to live and work in line with your purpose.

1. Think of 5 experiences in your life when you were really "in your element" and being your authentic self

1	
2	
3	
4	
5	

2. What was your highest intention at these times?

1	
2	
3	
4	
5	

3. Looking at the list above, what is a common theme revealed by your answers that points towards your higher purpose?

Higher Purpose	

4. Identify your next smallest step.

Next Step	

BUILD YOUR SUPPORT TEAM

We very rarely achieve our goals on our own, and usually for every successful person there is a team of people who have made it possible.

> "When I was out there I was never ever alone, there was always a team of people behind me, in mind if not in body"
>
> Ellen Mcarthur

Assemble your internal and external team by answering these questions - it's OK if the same name crops up in a few boxes. Take the time to talk to each person and explain how they can support you to achieve your goal. Explain to them how grateful you are for their support so far and the difference it has made to you.

Who can help you learn from your failures and successes?

Who can you turn to when you need support?

Who can you learn from who has been there and done that?

Who can inspire you?

Who can coach you to get the skills you need to achieve your goal?

Who can coach you to get the attitude you need to achieve your goal?

Who can you be honest with about the highs and lows?

Who else do you need on your team?

Who do you have on your inner support team

Who else do you have on your inner support team

TAKE ACTION NOW!

Beware of falling into the trap of waiting for things to happen for you – if you want something to happen, you have got to make it happen.

> *"Learning only happens when behaviour changes"*
>
> Wyatt Woodsmall

For example, if you are the Skipper of a yacht bound toward new lands, your first step is to cast off and leave port. As Skipper you must constantly evaluate progress in order to be sure you are on target. Unforeseen obstacles are sure to arise, such as a rainstorm, or increased southerly winds. As a result, to keep on course you may have to increase speed or guide the boat in a more westerly direction.

- Notice what is working and what is not working.
- If something is working, keep doing it!
- If an approach is not working, do something different.

Motivating Action

Once your client has identified their next smallest step, applying the SCORE model can help them focus on the positive effects and resources they have in order to take action.

1. *What is the next smallest step to take that will keep you moving forward?*

2. *What led you to choose that particular step as the next one to take?*

3. *What is your goal by taking this step?*

4. *What emotional states, beliefs or support do you need to take this step?*

5. *What will be the long term effect of taking this step?*

Learning from Perceived Failure

If a person has a useful strategy for celebrating and learning from their actions, they are more likely to do something where the results are uncertain. The SCORE model can provide a very useful framework for helping someone shift attention from the negative aspects of not getting the result they wanted on to the positive aspects of what they did.

1. *Tell me about what happened...*

2. *What do you appreciate or like about the things you did?*

3. *What might you do differently in the future?*

4. *What support and resources do you need / would you like?*

5. *What is the next smallest step to take that will keep you moving forward?*

11

Coaching

Programmes

"You are the person who has to decide. Whether you'll do it or toss it aside; you are the person who makes up your mind. Whether you'll lead or will linger behind. Whether you'll try for the goal that's afar. Or just be contented to stay where you are"

Edgar A. Guest

DELIVERING COACHING

Coaching can be delivered in many different ways. In general I have found that whatever the client's specific outcome the overall sequence and flow of coaching can remain relatively consistent. Two approaches are:

Informal Coaching

Informal, ad-hoc or 'stealth' coaching occurs when an opportunity arises for a person to use a coaching approach with another person or group. Informal coaching could happen over a chat by the coffee machine, as a hidden structure in running a meeting, chatting with a friend about a challenge they are having at work or when reviewing performance with a sportsman or team.

Get Commitment
- The coaching topic usually follows from the current conversation. Gain agreement for coaching by asking "Do you want to explore _____ for the next few minutes?"

Conversational Coaching Process
- S - "Tell me about the situation from your point of view"
- C - "How did it come about?"
- O - "What's your goal now?"
- R - "What skills, abilities and support do you have or can get?"
- E - "What do you need to do next to apply the resources towards your goal?"

Feedback and Evaluation
- Ask "how has this been helpful?" and use self-reflection and supervision to develop as a coach and improve your coaching skills and effectiveness.

Formal Coaching Session

I define formal coaching as anytime when a coach and a client come together at a scheduled time for the specific purpose of coaching. The coaching topic may be planned in advance or emergent in the session.

Identify Session Coaching Theme

- Identify the coaching theme for the session and define the evidence procedure that will let you know when you have achieved the overall coaching outcome.

Get Commitment

- Set boundaries for the coaching relationship and contract for an appropriate amount of time - either for one session or a set number of sessions

Conversational Coaching Process

- Using the SCORE model as a framework, explore fully the situation, cause and outcome for the client. Take your time to ensure you have discovered the most appropriate area for them to make a change (a state, a belief, a pattern or behaviour) and have a defined clear vision of how they want to be different.
- Use questions, metaphors, tasks and exercises to assist the client to recognise and gather the resources needed to make the change they want to improve their performance.

Agreed Actions for Client

- Fully explore the effects of applying the resources - future pace the positive changes and identify actions for the client to take.
- Consider agreeing a task to complete that supports the desired changes.

Feedback and Evaluation

- Ask for feedback from the client and use self-reflection and supervision to develop as a coach and improve your coaching skills and effectiveness.

COACHING PROGRAMMES

A coaching programme can last for any number of sessions, though a usual amount may be between 3 and 8. The sessions can be weekly or fortnightly when addressing a specific change or perhaps spread out over a period of up to a year to support ongoing development towards world class performance.

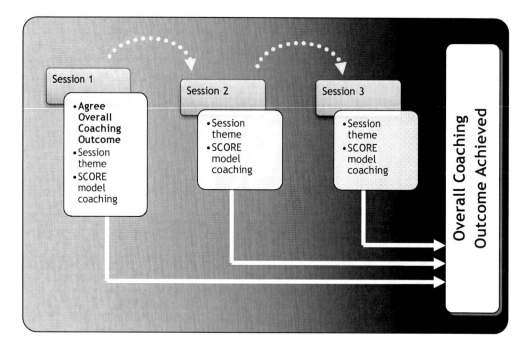

Emergent Coaching Programmes

Coaching on an emergent basis begins with the client and coach agreeing the overall theme and evidence criteria at the first session. Each session then takes a theme based on the current situation for the client with the overall outcome in mind. The coach uses their skills and talents to help the client meet their goals for each session.

Designed Coaching Programmes

Coaching may also be provided with a designed programme or theme for a set number of sessions. Within each session the coaching conversation is focussed on a topic of benefit to the client and the client identifies their current situation, a desired outcome or developmental goal within the topic and the resources they have or can get to help them achieve that outcome.

Example Coaching Programmes

These two examples illustrate how some of the topics in the book can be combined to sequence a coaching programme:

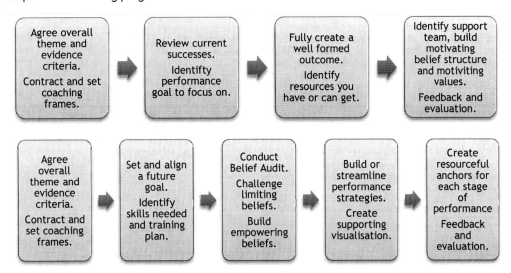

Using Tasks to Support the Programme

Coaching does not have to be confined to the coaching conversation and as well as the actions identified by the client to carry out between sessions, the coach may also suggest tasks to complete. These tasks work best when they direct a client to carrying out behaviours or actions that will support their understanding of themselves and achieving their goal. The possibilities are endless, however some examples to consider are.

HIGH PERFORMANCE

Performance psychologists working with many world class competitors and successful Olympic athletes suggest there are a number of mental factors that are common to all successful performers. By developing your mental strength you can make the most of your physical capability and technical skills.

Whether you want to perform at your best as a coach or help your clients perform at their best at work, at home or in their hobbies and interests, a balanced attitude and the following six factors will support high performance in any field.

Strong Desire

If you talk with anyone who has achieved a world class standard in what they do, their desire to succeed will shine through. They often describe how their preparation and training had a sense of purpose and they really wanted to perform to their potential. A strong motivation and desire helps you get the most from every moment.

- Do you know where you are going and how you are going to get there?
  - *Identify clear performance goals and plans to get you where you want to go*
- How much do you want to succeed and achieve your potential?
  - *Connect your performance with your motivating values and higher purpose*

Self Belief

All world class performance and competition brings expectation and pressure both from yourself or others. A strong self belief gives you the capacity to commit to practice hard and perform well under challenging situations. When things go wrong, self belief helps you to refocus and deal with whatever comes up in a confident and controlled manner.

- How good are you at staying positive under pressure?
  - *Create an empowering belief set to support you to perform at your best*
- Can you recover and come back stronger when things aren't going to plan?
  - *Build your self-efficacy so you can cope with all eventualities*

Focus *on What Matters*

There are always parts of preparation, training and performance that will be within your influence, and some parts that are not. Worrying about what you can't control wastes time and valuable energy. Instead of getting frustrated or delayed by poor weather, noise, distractions or equipment focus on what matters – your performance.

- How good are you at focusing your attention on what matters?
  - *Know your strengths and how you can apply them to perform at your best*
- How aware are you of the things you can influence and the things you can't?
  - *Identify what you need to pay attention to, and when you need to do it*

Positive Emotion

At any moment, your emotional state drives your behaviour - if you feel good you perform well and if you don't feel good, your performance level drops. Your mind and body are linked and everything you do conveys messages about confidence, commitment, motivation and attitude. Your physiology affects your thinking processes and emotional states.

- Do you approach every stage of performance in the right emotional state?
  - *Build resourceful emotional states and collapse un-resourceful anchors*
- Can you maintain positive body language when the challenge is hardest?
  - *Develop awareness of the link between your physiology and emotional states*

Strategies *for Success*

Most high performance strategies are unconscious, they run automatically and are the result of many hours of deliberate practice. The strategies people use at a world class level are usually different to the ones they used when first learning a skill. Take the time to refine your current strategies so that you are ready to cope with every eventuality in the best possible way.

- Do you know your strategies for when things go well, and when they don't?
  - *Identify and streamline your strategies for all phases of performance*
- Are you able to change strategies when you need to?
  - *Visualise yourself using successful strategies at challenging times*

Learning *Mindset*

Everything we do brings results and the ability to learn from your successes and failures will allow you to give yourself a break when things don't go well and congratulate yourself when things are a triumph. Take time to reflect on your preparation, training and performance and take a break with family, friends and other interests to maintain a balanced outlook.

- Can you enjoy learning from your past successes and failures?
  - *Adopt a growth mindset and use reflection and self coaching to develop*
- Can you take time out from your training to enjoy other aspects of your life?
  - *Build your support team and take the time to show gratitude for all they do*

Using the approaches detailed in this book and working with a mentor or coach is a very effective way to help a person improve in one or more of these areas. For more information I recommend "The Mental Game Plan" by Stephen Bull, John Albinson and Chris Shambrook and "In Pursuit of Excellence" by Terry Orlick.

STAGES OF BEHAVIOURAL CHANGE

The Trans-Theoretical Model of Behaviour Change (TTM) describes a 6 stage process where, for people to make a positive change, they must develop the right approach, attitudes and beliefs to embrace it. James Prochaska and Carlo DiClementi introduced the model in 1983 after much research to describe how people go about changing their health or lifestyle. Each of the stages depicts a distinct attitude and action for behaviour change.

1. Oblivious - Not even considering change yet - everything is 'fine' and the person is not aware of any alternatives.

2. Contemplation - Not changing, but thinking about it. In two minds about whether to stay as they are or try something new.

3. Preparation - Intending to change and making some small changes in first month or so. Not yet fully committed.

4. Action - Actively changing and practising the new behaviours for 3 - 6 months. Actioning the change is an all consuming activity.

5. Maintenance - Keeping the changes going for over 6 months as the change is integrated into the person's life.

6. Termination or Relapse - Either the new behaviour is as automatic as the old one used to be and a new identity is established or they return to the old behaviours because they have not yet made the necessary motivation, strategy or lifestyle adjustments for long term success. Relapse is a natural and integral part of the change process.

How Change Happens through the Model

In general, for people to progress through the stages of the model they need a growing awareness that the advantages of changing outweigh the disadvantages (the pros outweigh the cons); confidence that they can make and maintain changes in situations that tempt them to return to their old, unwanted behaviour (high self-efficacy); and strategies that can help them make and maintain change.

The type of strategies needed to assist people to change will depend on their current stage of change. For example, if you help a client to create a plan to follow, they will only adopt the new plan if they are at the preparation or action stages. If your client is only at the contemplation stage they will be unlikely to follow their new plan and a better approach is helping them decide that making a change is important, beneficial and achievable.

Concluding the Change

The theory acknowledges human frailty and the fact many people relapse at some stage. One study found that smokers trying to quit went through the cycle on average three or four times before they succeeded. Rather than abandoning the change altogether, **a relapse should be thought of as integral to the change process** and an opportunity to reassess if the strategies adopted fit with your lifestyle. In fact it is only by going through the experience of relapse can a person fully learn what they need to learn to make the changes they want.

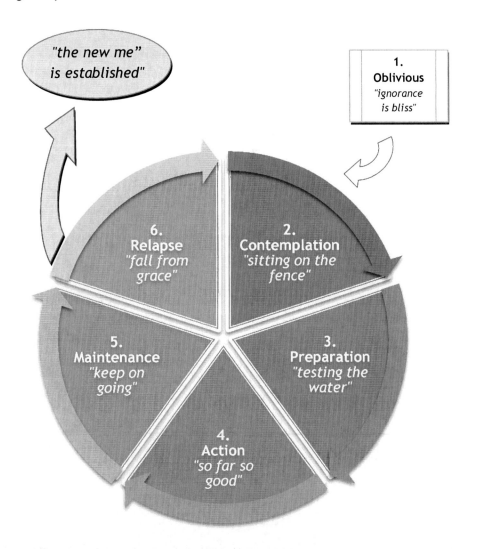

"the new me"
is established"

1.
Oblivious
"ignorance
is bliss"

6.
Relapse
"fall from
grace"

2.
Contemplation
"sitting on the
fence"

5.
Maintenance
"keep on
going"

3.
Preparation
"testing the
water"

4.
Action
"so far so
good"

COACHING BEHAVIOURAL CHANGE

The TTM of Change is a very useful framework for assessing where you client is in their process of change and clarifying the boundaries of your coaching relationship. The coaching may be a single session aimed at helping them improve their performance within the stage of change they are at. The coaching may be a longer term assignment aimed at supporting them through several or even all of the stages of change.

- What stage of change is your client at?
- Is their coaching outcome compatible with their stage of behavioural change?
- What stage in the cycle have you contracted to help your client achieve?
- What stage of change are you at as a coach?

Stage of Change	Some options to consider as a coach
Pre-contemplation	People at this stage are likely to underestimate the Pros of changing and overestimate the Cons. Offer appropriate information as to why change may be helpful, and encourage the client to think about the subject, become well-informed and take responsibility for where they are now.
Contemplation The pros balance the cons and the person may keep putting off taking action or be locked into looking for the perfect solution before acting.	• Explore the consequences of the pattern of staying the same • Explore ecology - benefits and drawbacks of change • Consider small ways they could begin to make changes • Look at ways of reducing the cons of changing their behaviour • Build awareness of all the resources they have or can get • Connect to motivating values and empowering beliefs • Learn about the kind of person they could be if they changed
Preparation People may be concerned that when they act, they may fail. Help them to build a strong support team and make solid preparations to keep progressing.	• Recall previous evidence of success • Visualise and connect to the feelings of the future outcome state • Break the plan down into achievable goals • Make aware of Bandura Dip to counter anxiety • Build empowering beliefs and change limiting beliefs • Build a support team of family and friends • Set resourceful anchors

Stage of Change	Some options to consider as a coach
Action Help people to strengthen their commitments to change and to fight urges to slip back through building positive behaviours and celebrating successes	• Follow the plan, monitor and review progress • Reward and congratulate successes (even small successes) • Teach relaxation response to balance activity of new behaviour • Create helpful anchors, collapse unhelpful anchors • Explore what's working and do even more of it • Explore what's not working and do less of it or change it • Model others who have done it and get mentors to support and guide
Maintenance Assist people to be aware of potentially tempting situations and maintain new strategies and behaviours with the support of mentors and others.	• Continue to celebrate ongoing successes • Avoid people, places and pressures that can compromise the change • Find a way to use your experience to help others make changes • Streamline strategies of excellence • Build metaphors for the future identity • Learn from mentors and people who have achieved the same change • Explore what is now possible for you with the new behaviour
Relapse Encourage people to see perceived failure as valuable feedback. Help them consider even more benefits of making the change now.	• Remind of previous positive experiences • See it as taking one step back to take two steps forward • Build new resourceful states and strategies and beliefs • Explore the learnings – it's OK to fail • Remind that it's normal for people to need more than one attempt • Be prepared to budget more time, energy and money for the change • Set a new goal given what you now know

IDENTITY LEVEL CHANGE

Who we are is constantly changing and updating with our every experience. Over the years philosophers, psychologists and psychotherapists have recognised we hold within us a sense of self, and have also discussed and argued about exactly what the "self" is and how it is formed. From a NLP perspective we are less concerned with a theory of why, but we are curious in modelling how a person expresses, maintains and changes their sense of self.

Our identity represents our concept of who we are and the roles we have in our life. Identity is who we are when we express our map of the world. For example if my map contains information about being a loving, caring father who shares the housework and childcare then I may take on the identity of being a "Modern Man." If my map contains ideas

that the Father works hard to earn the money, Mother takes care of the children and children are best seen and not heard then I may adopt the identity of a "Traditional Father." Similarly at work, a persons map of the world may express itself in the identity of "caring boss," "team-worker," "troublemaker" or even "tyrant."

Some of the elements that make up our concept of who we are include meta-programs, memories, values, beliefs, skills and behaviour. When coaching if we help a client make a change in any one of these areas we can facilitate a person in updating their map of the world and their identity to one that provides even more choice and freedom in response to the certain uncertainty of life.

Meta-programs

Meta-programs are filtering systems that direct the habitual ways we gather information, make decisions and responses and evaluate situations.

- By changing the filtering systems we use we can change our experience of the world and update how we operate in the world.

Memories

Memories provide the evidence for our belief and value systems to maintain their structure. They may be of events that contain significant emotions or decisions that have shaped, confirmed or changed our map of the world.

- Leaving the past in the past and letting go of any baggage allows people to be themselves in the here and now.

Beliefs

Beliefs tend to filter those things that we can/can't or will/won't do in life. They have a direct effect on behaviour and shape our perceptions of the world - if we believe that something is a certain way then we will filter our experiences to prove to ourselves that it is so. Core beliefs are usually held unconsciously and shape our whole life-style.

- Ensuring a person has resourceful core beliefs will allow them to approach life with the freedom to go after and get whatever they truly want.

Values

Values define what is important to us and are the basis for how we evaluate the events we experience. In general, a person's value set should reflect where they are now and where they want to be in the future.

- Resolving past values that have been inherited or out of date will give a person greater determination and motivation to act in ways that express their true self.

Skills

Our capability and skills are the result of conscious practice and unconscious modelling. As humans we are natural learning machines and the skills we have are constantly available for updating, if we know how and take action to do it.

- Helping a person embrace a growth mindset and learn new skills, states and strategies will enable them to take risks, flourish and grow.

Behaviour

Our behaviour represents what we are doing and saying at any moment - both in the outside world and our inside world. NLP can help people become aware of and directly influence the internal representations that drive their emotional states and actions.

- Taking control of their internal representations gives a person the ability to choose their experiences and responses to external events.

Coaching is generally concerned with helping clients make changes that fit their identity. Changes made in one area may well affect other areas of a persons life - increased confidence at work may lead to increased confidence at home or at club meetings. Identity level change occurs when this reaches a threshold (time or quantity) and they upgrade their identity from *"I am a shy person"* to *"I am a confident person"*.

WHAT TO USE WHEN

This list is a guide – it is not designed to represent the best or the only options you have. It is a merely an indication of some of your options of how using what is covered in this book can help your client access the resources they need to make the changes they want.

The patterns represent one way to apply the fundamental NLP tools and approach. Every client, every NLP coach and every situation is different. Use what you think is the most appropriate technique and calibrate to your client. If it works, great. If another approach seems best to go with, do that. The learning is in the experience!

Emotional states

When a client is not feeling how they want to in a situation

- The resource triangle
- Shifting perceptual positions
- The relaxation response
- Strategies of excellence
- Anchoring desired state

When a client wants to access helpful emotional states

- The resource triangle
- Progressive relaxation routine
- Anchoring desired state
- Strategies of excellence
- Future pacing desired state

Beliefs

When a client wants to overcome limiting beliefs

- Reframing to change beliefs
- Belief change cycle
- Shifting perceptual positions
- Values ladder
- Reversal questions

When a client wants a set of empowering beliefs

- Building empowering beliefs
- Assessing beliefs about a goal
- Building self-efficacy
- The resource triangle
- Metaphors for a change

Thinking patterns

When a client wants to resolve stuck or circular thinking

- Framing questions
- Reversal questions
- Reframing
- Shifting perceptual positions
- Exploring and changing patterns

When a client wants to create or discover new approaches

- Exploring and changing patterns
- Strategies of excellence
- Dancing SCORE
- New behaviour generator
- Metaphors for a change

Behaviours

When a client wants to stop procrastination or unhelpful actions

- Identifying the real goal
- Values ladder
- Exploring and changing patterns
- The resource triangle
- Framing questions

When a client wants to create motivation to carry out wanted behaviours

- New behaviour generator
- Visualising success
- Connecting to motivating values
- Building empowering beliefs
- Dancing SCORE

Goals

When a client wants to explore their goals

- Key area goals
- Primary energy goals
- Performance and end goals
- Achievement goals
- NLP Logical Levels goals
- Listening and precision model questions

Performance

When a client want to improve their performance level

- Identifying the real goal
- Connecting to motivating values
- Assessing and strengthening belief
- Building self-efficacy
- Anchoring desired states
- New behaviour generator
- Visualising success

Other NLP patterns that are helpful in coaching:

- Collapsing Anchors, Chaining Anchors
- Sub-modality Map Across and Belief Change
- Swish Pattern
- Phobia Model
- Sleight of Mouth Belief Change Patterns
- Meta Programs – Language and Behaviour Profile
- Parts Integration
- 6-Step Reframe
- Timeline belief change
- Timeline accessing resources
- Timeline clearing block from the past
- Values elicitation and alignment

12

Development
as a Coach

---

*"Learning is the process whereby knowledge is
created through the transformation of experience"*

David A Kolb

LEARNING FROM EXPERIENCE

The ability to learn from experiences where you have adopted a coaching approach is an essential part of being a reflexive coach. A useful description of how the process of learning from experience happens is described by David Kolb in four stages:

- Concrete Experience
  Actively engaged and **doing**

- Reflective Observation
  Reviewing and replaying the experience

- Abstract Conceptualisation
  Concluding by linking concepts, meaning and theory

- Active Experimentation
  Planning how to apply the new learning

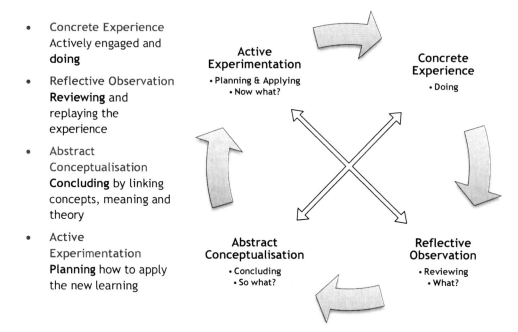

Active Experimentation
• Planning & Applying
• Now what?

Concrete Experience
• Doing

Abstract Conceptualisation
• Concluding
• So what?

Reflective Observation
• Reviewing
• What?

Learning from experience

Sometime a person has a preference for one or two of the stages more than the others. Often people may have been trying to learn from their situation or solve a problem using only a pair of the stages. Focussing on perceptions (doing and concluding) or internal processing (reviewing and planning) can lead to limited learning. Restoring the missing stages can help a person fully learn and develop from experience.

For example: a person may be experiencing conflict with their boss (concrete experience) and decide that means that the boss is hard headed and uncaring (abstract conceptualisation). Their conclusion then informs the next meeting with the boss and the conflict is perceived to continue or even get worse. By reviewing and replaying the experience (reflective observation) and planning and applying a new response (active experimentation) the person can truly learn from their experience and enjoy new choices in that situation.

Self Supervision Questions

As a coach, ensuring you consider your experience in each of the four ways can help you develop further. The example questions are also a useful set for helping a client recognise their own learning from an experience.

Concrete Experience (Doing)	Reflective Observation (Reflecting)	Abstract Conceptualisation (Concluding)	Active Experimentation (Applying)
Being in the moment as a coach and using your sensory awareness (what you are seeing, hearing and feeling) to guide your approach. Using 1st, 2nd and 3rd position to gather additional information and self-supervise in the moment.	What actually happened?	What process did the coaching follow?	What would you like to keep on doing?
	What were your feelings at the time?	What approaches could you have used?	What would you like to do differently?
	What worked?	What theories or models describe what happened?	How will you use this knowledge in the future?
	What didn't work so well?	How did what you did influence the client?	Where can you apply your learnings?
	What skills, techniques or attitudes did you use?	What patterns did you recognise in yourself?	When will you use your new learnings?

NLP Coach Skills Self Assessment

The ability to be critical about your thoughts, actions and feelings will allow you to evaluate what works and identify areas for your development. Rate yourself against the following skills on a regular basis.

	My general assessment of my competence (✓)			Contexts where I find this challenging	How I am going to improve in this area
	Could improve	OK	Very Good		
Assessment of my ability as a NLP Coach					
Work within an outcome frame					
Operate ethically with a positive intent for you, client(s) and the wider world					
Establish and maintain states of resourcefulness in yourself					
Establish and maintain states of resourcefulness with your client					
Establish and maintain suitable levels of rapport					
Sort by others (work with the other person or groups best interest in mind)					
Respect, pace and work within other people's models of the world					
Perform effective and ecological change work					
To elicit the states and responses you are after within both yourself and others					

EXAMPLE REFLECTIVE JOURNAL

Keeping a journal of your learning and coaching practice, as you develop as a coach, will help you to see trends in your coaching and provide a useful reference for your supervision sessions.

Name _____

Date _____

The main points I have learnt from the session are:

•

How I could develop my practical coaching skills as a result of the session:

•

How I could develop my knowledge and understanding as a coach as a result of the session:

•

SUPERVISION

Coach supervision and mentoring is an opportunity for active coaches to step outside their coaching relationships and focus on developing their effectiveness.

- The primary purpose of supervision is to support the coach to explore and develop their working practice leading to the best possible service to clients.

Some of the benefits of supervision are:

- Discovering new ways of working
- Getting feedback on your coaching
- Reflecting on your work with your clients
- Deepening your knowledge and wisdom
- Aligning with professional standards and ethics
- Understanding yourself and your coaching approach
- Resolving difficulties or challenges with clients
- Improving your effectiveness
- Learning new approaches

The Focus in Supervision

The 7-eyed model of supervision from Peter Hawkins and Robin Shohet is a useful model that defines 7 areas of focus. Each supervision meeting may consider one or several of these areas in order to help you be more effective as a coach.

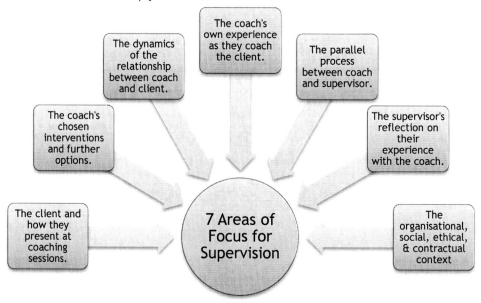

Types of Supervision

The best type and frequency of supervision is that which suits you and your needs. There are three main options:

- Individual - 1:1 either face to face or by telephone / skype with a supervisor
- Supervised Group - the supervisor directs the process and keeps the sessions purposeful and effective
- Peer Group - a number of similarly experienced coaches come together to facilitate peer learning

Self supervision supports all these formal options. This happens in the session (when you take a 3rd Position to what is going on) and following sessions where you reflect on the experience and make links to what you already know and what development needs you have. It is a very beneficial skill to develop and working with a supervisor in the first instance can help you develop and improve your self-supervision skills in a coaching context.

Do I need Supervision?

That is of course a question that only you can answer since you know how much experience you have, how much coaching you provide and what coaching topics you deal with. What I can say is that if coaching supervision supports you to explore and develop your working practice leading to the best possible service to clients, why would you not? Check if your employer or the coaching organisation you have joined requires or advises regular supervision.

- If you were working with a coach, would you expect them to be supervised?

Selecting a Supervisor

It is helpful to select a supervisor who can support and challenge you, helping you see any blind spots and guide your ongoing development as a coach. A few aspects to consider are:

- They have experience as a coach
- They have experience as a supervisor and supervisee
- They have a clear theoretical framework for their own practice
- They follow a clear theoretical and ethical framework
- They are committed to CPD

- They have the knowledge and experience to deepen understanding of yourself and your practice
- They have an understanding of the context in which you are a coach
- They don't have a dual role (i.e. not also line manager, business partner, close friend, etc.)

13

The Business of Coaching

"If one advances confidently in the direction of his dreams, and endeavours to live the life which he has imagined, he will meet with a success unexpected in common hours"

Henry David Thoreau

OPERATING AS A COACH

NLP Coaching

Firstly when you are operating as a coach, it is important to remember NLP Coaching is an educational approach and is not therapy, counselling, or consulting, nor is it a substitute for them. NLP Coaching is outcome focussed and can help your client address:

Emotional states	Thinking patterns
• not feeling how they want to in a situation • wanting to access helpful emotions	• resolving stuck or circular thinking • discovering new strategies

Beliefs	Repeating behaviours
• overcoming limiting beliefs • building empowering beliefs	• stopping procrastination or unhelpful actions • creating motivation for new behaviours

"One thing that people really need to get about my life's work is that it's not about therapy or business or 'networking' organisations - it's about freedom." Richard Bandler

Marketing Yourself

Marketing is the process of matching what you want to provide with the needs of the people who will buy your product or service. To succeed in business as a coach you will need to stand out from the crowd. Are you a business coach, a sports coach, a life coach, a personal development coach, a leadership coach, a confidence coach, or a different kind of coach?

- What is your definition of coaching?
- What are the benefits of coaching?

Firstly consider your clients, who do you want to coach and what makes you sure you have the skills and experience to help them achieve their goals?

- What problems will coaching with you solve?
- What solutions will coaching with you provide?

Within the field of coaching there are many people that are able to help others, but nobody can do exactly what you do. If you met someone in a lift and they asked *"What do you do?"* what would you say? How would you convey your energy, style and approach?

- What makes you unique?

Professional Bodies that Relate to Coaching

There are many professional bodies and learning organisations that offer coaching training and self accredited programmes. (A search on the internet will deliver 22 million results for "coaching training").

The International NLP Trainers Association has well respected certification programmes at Coach Practitioner and Master Coach levels. If you are serious in applying NLP in coaching I strongly recommend enhancing your skills on one of these trainings. Find out more at www.inlpta.org and www.valleytraining.co.uk

Accreditation

Three coaching organisations you could consider joining are the EMCC, AfC and ICF. Each have active networks and run a programme of CPD events as well as comprehensive accreditation processes.

European Mentoring and Coaching Council   *Association for Coaching*   *International Coach Federation*

Accreditation bodies require a course of coach specific training covering the core competencies of coaching plus a significant number of coaching documented hours. Look at each organisations website to discover their specific requirements at each level and start logging each coaching session now!

Which one do I join?

This is a common discussion on my coach training courses and the best advice came from a participant a few years ago who was an experienced coach already (but new to NLP) and suggested considering the following questions:

- How important is accreditation to you?
- Do you need a way to convey credibility as a coach?
- Which organisation(s) does your sponsor or client recognise?
- Is the programme of CPD events accessible and relevant to you?
- Is there a fit between the organisations purpose and values and your own?

SETTING BOUNDARIES

Coaching Agreements

The precise nature and format of your coaching agreement is up to you and should be drawn up to reflect the coaching that you provide. For those people involved in corporate programmes they might benefit from an 'industry standard' commercial Coaching Agreement drawn up by the EMCC and ICF. Your supervisor will be able to help you prepare a suitable agreement for your work as a coach. Typically it will cover:

- What is Involved
- Your Style and Approach
- Client Responsibilities
- Coach Responsibilities
- Record Keeping
- Appointments
- Cancellations
- Fees / Charges

- Overall programme, number of sessions, duration, location etc.
- Ending the Contract
- Confidentiality
- Recording of Sessions
- Supervision Arrangements
- Professional Memberships
- Ethical Considerations / Boundaries

The Coaching Location

For each client or group the coaching location may be different. In general it is best to avoid interruptions and be a setting where the client feels comfortable and able to talk freely about their situation. This could be in a private meeting room, an office, by the coffee machine, over the phone or out in the countryside.

- What elements make up a safe coaching environment for your clients?
- How can you adapt a given location to make it suitable for a coaching conversation?

Ethics

The major coaching organisations all have ethical codes of conduct and as a coach you may wish to be familiar with these and adopt one as the basis for your personal ethical code.

Supervision

Coaching supervision is highly recommended to ensure you are operating in the best way to meet your clients needs and to support your development as a coach. The precise type and frequency of supervision will be dictated by the type and quantity of coaching you provide and the requirements of any professional memberships. A potential supervisor will be able to advise you further.

When coaching may not be appropriate

These situations are offered as a guideline for when coaching may not the most appropriate approach to use. Ultimately as a coach, you must decide if you are working within safe boundaries - ask your supervisor for guidance if you are unsure.

If the person is resistant or closed to coaching.

Coaching is likely to be ineffective if the person is forced into coaching and has no interest in change or improvement. Ensure that coaching is presented as a generative approach aimed at bringing the best out of people.

If the person has a developmental need which is widely shared.

In this case a training course or development programme may be equally effective and possibly more cost-effective.

If the person has a personal or family crisis.

In this situation, the individual will benefit from support and somebody to talk to. A confidential therapeutic or counselling intervention is likely to be more appropriate.

If the person has identified psychological problems

For example anxiety, addiction, depression etc. In this case referral to an appropriate specialist like a psychotherapist is appropriate.

If the person continually engages in inappropriate/undesirable behaviour.

If the behaviour has become frequent and ingrained, coaching may not an appropriate intervention. Refer to a professional psychotherapist.

If you are close friend or relation

Generally work with your own family and spouse should be avoided as you might be part of the problem.

If the person is dangerous to self or others

If the presenting problem or the personal history that you gather from the client indicates to you that the client is dangerous to self or others or is looking for treatment for a physiological and for a life threatening disease, then the client is likely to be beyond the scope of coaching. Refer to a suitable professional.

If traumatic material is revealed during the coaching

Under certain circumstances, highly traumatic or repressed material could indicate that if you were not trained in interventions that are effective in this area it would be best to refer the client to a professional psychotherapist.

Questions a Client May Ask

It is reasonable for clients to assume that if they are coming to a professional coach, then that person has all the skills and abilities required to help them move forward in the right way for them. In practice it's very unlikely you will ever be asked all these questions however, to increase your confidence as a coach it may be helpful to consider your answers.

Your coaching approach
- Why are you a coach?
- How do you define coaching?
- How do you describe your coaching style?
- What benefits do you think coaching offers?
- What is your particular area of focus in coaching?
- What tools/techniques/models do you like to use?
- Can you describe the theoretical framework you use for the coaching you deliver?
- How do you suggest I/we should evaluate the success of the coaching process?
- What is your preferred coaching format - face to face, phone, skype?
- How do you select coaching clients?
- Do you ever turn away potential clients? If so, for what reasons?

Previous coaching experience
- How long have you worked as a coach?
- In what kinds of organisations and industry sectors have you worked?
- At what levels in an organisation have you worked?
- How many hours of coaching have you delivered?
- How many clients have you worked with?
- What kinds of issues/problems have you coached individuals on?
- Have you experience of team coaching?

References
- Are you able to provide references from previous clients?

Qualifications/training

- What training/qualifications have you undertaken relating to your coaching practice?
- Please describe any development activities you have undertaken in the past year as continuing professional development?
- Do you use any psychometric tests to support your coaching?

Relevant experience

- Please describe your business experience?
- What experience/understanding do you have of the [specific organisation/industry] environment?
- What experience do you have of working with 3 corned (coach, client, organisation) and 4 corned contracts (coach, client, HR, manager)?

Membership of professional bodies

- Are you a member of any professional bodies? If yes, at what level?
- Do you adhere to a code of ethics/conduct as part of your membership of a professional body?

Professional indemnity insurance

- Do you hold professional indemnity insurance?
- If yes, with whom and to what level?

Supervision

- How do you maintain your objectivity and perspective during coaching assignments?
- What activities do you undertake to keep your skills up to date and ensure you are keeping abreast of professional developments in the field of coaching?
- Do you think supervision is important for coaching professionals?
- Do you have your own coach or supervisor?

EXAMPLE COACHING RECORD

Keeping a record of a coaching session is essential to allow you to easily recall progress. You may prefer to complete the summary information as you go along or at the close of each session. Keep all your coaching records in accordance with the Data Protection Act.

Name _____

Date _____

Present State

```



```

Coaching Notes

s

c

o

r

e

Agreed Actions

```



```

YOUR COACHING PROFILE

Marketing is the fundamental starting point of any business and successfully applying your coaching skills will be a combination of 7 elements. Whether you are running a coaching business or coaching others as part of your job role knowing your coaching profile will help you be clear about the coaching you can provide.

In marketing terms, coaching is a service - the action of doing something for someone. This provides some unique challenges in how you operate:

- How will you convey evidence of the quality of your coaching?
- How can you ensure consistency between sessions?
- How can you create and deliver effective coaching sessions in the moment?

The American railroad industry struggled because it considered itself in the railroad business rather than in the transportation business (Levitt, 1960). This fundamental shift in business definition would have dictated a very different approach to planning, growth and ultimately the long life of the industry. **What business are you in as a coach?**

BUSINESS START-UP TIPS

Thinking of starting a new business as a coach can be an exciting time. There are many helpful sources of information on the internet, in the UK a very good starting point is http://www.businesslink.gov.uk

Here are a few ideas to begin with. This is by no means an exhaustive list, but may help you to start turning your dream towards a possible reality.

1. **Think about your goals.**

   What are you setting out to achieve? How big are your goals right now - are they realistic goals or dreams. Use the Disney Creativity Strategy for yourself.

   Write your goals down - commit what you want to paper and ensure that your goal is aligned with all areas of you and your life.

2. **Why are you setting up in business?**

   You need to ask yourself if you are the right person to start a coaching business. What do you ultimately want from your coaching business? What is the bigger purpose? Do you have the skills and temperament to be a good coach and a good business owner?

3. **What will happen if it doesn't work out?**

   Do you need a back-up plan to give you and your family security if it doesn't take off as fast as you wanted or is as successful as you expected? Are all your eggs in one basket?

4. **Research your market.**

   Make sure there is demand and also check pricing options. Talk to prospective clients - would they come to coaching, how much would they pay, what sort of programme would they like, what times, and (most importantly) what problems do they have that your coaching can provide solutions to.

   Pretend to be a coaching customer and ring up other coaches in the area. Find out what they do and how much they charge. Find your niche.

   Be realistic about the market.

5. **Decide where you are going to work.**

   Do you need separate premises for coaching or will you coach at your clients premises. Do you have space at home for a business office and / or coaching room?

   Many hotels offer meeting rooms for hire or a quiet corner in a large hotel may be appropriate for the coaching you offer. Perhaps renting a room at a complementary health centre would work for your clients.

   If you are going to offer coaching by phone or Skype do you have a quiet space to use in your home where you won't be disturbed?

6. **Get yourself a good coach**

    Get yourself a coach with whom you can explore your motivations and goals for setting up in business, and address any interference that will limit your potential.

7. **Find a business mentor.**

    Seek out the advice of a family friend who has the experience of being in business, or someone who is recommended to you, or someone you are close to. Perhaps an accountant or someone from the local enterprise agency. In the UK Business Link (www.businesslink.gov.uk) have some great guides and advice on what you need to do.

8. **Involve your family?**

    If you have a husband or wife or children, involving them in the decision to go it alone is important. Your home atmosphere should be very supportive, particularly in the early stages. Your family could also be useful as a sounding board, helping out with the odd task or providing feedback or finance.

9. **Be honest about your weaknesses**

    Identify what you do well and what you do badly, dividing it into areas such as financial, marketing and general management. Be honest with yourself, but also be realistic. Try and get someone else to evaluate your answers – another person's perspective can be very valuable. Identifying your weakness will help you to recognise what you are good at, and which areas you will need to find someone who can do a better job than you.

10. **Make sure you know how you are going to finance your new business.**

    Are you going "all-in" or starting the business in addition to your current work? Dipping your toe in means you can test your idea out without risking everything. You can carry on earning money from your job while you are starting up. Use your spare time to carry out your market research.

    Have you plans to survive the first 3-6 months whatever happens?

11. **Be legal.**

    Let the Inland Revenue and National Insurance Offices know if you are going to begin working as self employed in addition to your current job (there is a simple form to complete).

    Consider finding an accountant for advice on bookkeeping. Keep all your business transactions separate from your personal ones.

12. **Get insured**

    It is strongly advised to have professional indemnity insurance for Coaching. Membership of a professional body may entitle you to a discount.

13. **Write a thorough Business Plan.**

References & Bibliography

TOOLS & TECHNIQUES REFERENCE

This is not an exhaustive list but you may find it a useful start if you would like to explore some of the references for this book or read more in the classic texts that introduce the field of NLP.

NLP Skill, Tool or Technique	Read More In	Authors
The Map is Not the Territory	The Structure of Magic I P7	Bandler and Grinder
NLP Communication Model	Timeline Therapy and The Basis of Personality P3	Woodsmall and James
The Importance of State	Timeline Therapy and The Basis of Personality P9	Woodsmall and James
Conscious and Unconscious	Frogs into Princes P37 Training Trances P2	Bandler and Grinder Overdurf and Silverthorn
Being at Cause	The Structure of Magic I P51	Bandler and Grinder
Congruence	The Structure of Magic II P45 Reframing P179	Bandler and Grinder Bandler and Grinder
Ecology	Frogs into Princes P149	Bandler and Grinder
Sensory Acuity	Frogs into Princes P17	Bandler and Grinder
Hallucination	The Structure of Magic II P32	Bandler and Grinder
Calibration	Trance-formations P201	Bandler and Grinder
Rapport	Magic NLP Demystified P65	Lewis and Pucelik
Pacing and Leading	Patterns of the Hypnotic Techniques of Milton H. Erickson I P137 Frogs into Princes P80	Bandler and Grinder Bandler and Grinder
Sequencing	Reframing P153	Bandler and Grinder
Therapeutic Double Bind	The Structure of Magic I P169	Bandler and Grinder
Milton Model	Patterns of the Hypnotic Techniques of Milton H. Erickson P146	Bandler and Grinder
Meta Model	The Structure of Magic I P40	Bandler and Grinder
Well Formed Outcomes	Timeline Therapy and The Basis of Personality P80	Woodsmall and James
Representation Systems	The Structure of Magic II P6, 58 Magic NLP Demystified P31	Bandler and Grinder Lewis and Pucelik
Eye Accessing Cues	Frogs into Princes P25	Bandler and Grinder

Overlapping	The Structure of Magic P23	Bandler and Grinder
Synaesthesia	NLP Volume 1 P23 The Structure of Magic II P101	Dilts, Grinder, Bandler, DeLozier Bandler and Grinder
Chunking	Timeline Therapy and The Basis of Personality P193	Woodsmall and James
Anchoring	Frogs into Princes P82	Bandler and Grinder
Collapse Anchors	Frogs into Princes P106	Bandler and Grinder
Future Pacing	Frogs into Princes P87	Bandler and Grinder
Change Personal History	Frogs into Princes P108	Bandler and Grinder
Values	Timeline Therapy and The Basis of Personality P155	Woodsmall and James
Beliefs	Changing Belief Systems with NLP P20	Robert Dilts
Logical Levels	Changing Belief Systems with NLP P1	Robert Dilts
Alignment of Self	Visionary Leadership Skills P36	Robert Dilts
Metaphors	Therapeutic Metaphors P39	David Gordon
Perceptual Positions	Turtles all the Way Down P197 Using Your Brain for a Change P37	Grinder and DeLozier Richard Bandler
The Meta Mirror	Changing Belief Systems with NLP P198	Robert Dilts
Association and Disassociation	Using Your Brain for a Change P40	Richard Bandler
New Behaviour Generator	Transformations P178	Bandler and Grinder
Sub-modality Distinctions	The Insiders Guide to Sub- Modalities P46	Bandler & MacDonald
Sub-modality Map Across	The Insiders Guide to Sub- Modalities P13	Bandler & MacDonald
Sub-modality Belief Change	Using Your Brain for a Change P103	Richard Bandler
Phobia Model	Using Your Brain for a Change P43	Richard Bandler
Modelling	Timeline Therapy and The Basis of Personality P96	Woodsmall and James
Strategies	NLP Volume I P26	Dilts, Grinder, Bandler, DeLozier
Swish	Using Your Brain for a Change P131	Richard Bandler
In Time-Through time	Timeline Therapy and The Basis of Personality P23	Woodsmall and James

Clearing an Unwanted Emotion	Timeline Therapy and The Basis of Personality P87	Woodsmall and James
Linguistic Reframing	Reframing P9	Bandler and Grinder
6 Step Reframe	Reframing P114 Frogs into Princes P138	Bandler and Grinder Bandler and Grinder
Parts Integration	Reframing	Bandler and Grinder
Uptime and Downtime	Frogs into Princes P163	Bandler and Grinder
Hypnosis	Trance-formations P5	Bandler and Grinder
NLP Coaching Process	NLP Volume 1 P14	Dilts, Grinder, Bandler, DeLozier

References & Further Reading

This list includes the principle references referred to in the book plus some key texts that have influenced my thinking and practice in applying NLP to coaching. Please enjoy discovering something new with the wisdom of those who have already committed their thoughts to paper.

Alder, H. (1994) NLP, *The New Art and Science of Getting What You Want*, London: Judy Piakus

Alexander, G & Renshaw, B (2005) *Supercoaching, The Missing Ingredient for High Performance*, London: Random House

Andreas, C & Andreas, S (1987) *Change Your Mind - and Keep The Change*, Moab, UT: Real People Press

Andreas, C & Andreas, S (1989) *Heart of The Mind*, Moab, UT: Real People Press

Andreas, S & Faulkner, C (1996) *NLP The New Technology of Achievement*, London: Nicholas Brealey

Bandler, R. (1985) *Using Your Brain for a Change*, Moab, UT: Real People Press

Bandler, R. (1992) *Magic In Action*, Capitola, CA: Meta Publications

Bandler, R. (2008) *Richard Bandler's Guide to trance-formation*, Deerfield Beach, FL: Health Communications Inc

Bandler, R. & Grinder, J. (1975) *The Structure of Magic I: A Book about Language and Therapy*, Palo Alto, CA: Science and Behaviour Books

Bandler, R. & Grinder, J. (1975) *Patterns of the Hypnotic Techniques of Milton H. Erickson, M.D. Vol. I*, Cupertino, CA: Meta Publications

Bandler, R. & Grinder, J. (1979) *Frogs into Princes: Neuro-Linguistic Programming*, Moab, UT: Real People Press

Bandler, R. & Grinder, J. (1979) *ReFraming: Neuro-Linguistic Programming and the Transformation of Meaning*, Moab, UT: Real People Press

Bandler, R., Grinder, J & Satir, V. (1976) *Changing With Families, A Book about Further Education for Being Human*, Palo Alto, CA: Science and Behaviour Books

Bandler, R. & MacDonald, W. (1988) *An Insider's Guide to Sub-modalities*, Capitola, CA: Meta Publications

Bandura, A. (1977) *Self-efficacy: Toward a unifying theory of behaviour change.* Psychological Review, 84, (191-215).

Bateson, G. (1972) *Steps to an Ecology of Mind*, London: University of Chicago Press

Benson, H. (1975) *The Relaxation Response*, New York: Avon Books

Bull,S & Albinson, J & Shambrook, C (1996) *The Mental Game Plan*, Cheltenham: Sports Dynamics

Cameron-Bandler, L (1985) *Solutions, Enhancing Love, Sex and Relationships*, Moab, UT: Real People Press

Cameron-Bandler, L. Gordon, D. and Lebeau M. (1985) *Know How, Guided Programs For Inventing Your Best Future*, San Rafael, California: FuturePace Inc

Cameron-Bandler, L (1986) *The Emotional Hostage, Rescuing Your Emotional Life*, Moab, UT: Real People Press

Charvet, S (1995) *Words that Change Minds*, Dubuqe, IW: Kendall/Hunt

Churches, R and Terry, R. (2007) *NLP for Teachers: How to be a Highly Effective Teacher*, Carmarthen, Wales: Crown House Publishing

Dilts, R. (1990) *Changing Belief Systems with NLP*, Capitola CA: Meta Publications

Dilts, R. (1999) *Sleight of Mouth, The Magic of Conversational Belief Change*, Capitola CA: Meta Publications

Dilts, R., Grinder, J., Bandler, R., Delozier, J. (1980) *Neuro-linguistic Programming Volume I: The Study of the Structure of Subjective Experience*, Cupertino, CA: Meta Publications

Dilts, R. & Delozier, J. (1980) *Encyclopaedia of Systemic Neuro-Linguistic Programming and NLP New Coding*, Scotts Valley, CA: NLP University Press

Dweck, C. (2006). *Mindset, The New Psychology of Success.* Random House

Gallwey, T. (2000) *The Inner Game of Work: Overcoming mental obstacles for maximum performance*, Texere

Gallwey, T. (1975) *The Inner Game of Tennis*, Random House

Goleman, D. (1996) *Emotional Intelligence, Why It Can Matter More Than IQ*, London: Bloomsbury Books

Gordon, D. (1978) *Therapeutic Metaphors*, Capitola, CA: Meta Publications

Grinder, J. & Bandler, R. (1976) *The Structure of Magic II: A Book about Communication and Change*, Palo Alto, CA: Science and Behaviour Books

Grinder, J & Bandler, R. (1981) *TRANCE-Formations: Neuro-Linguistic Programming and the Structure of Hypnosis*, Moab, UT: Real People Press

Grinder, J & Bostic St. Clair. (2001) *Whispering In The Wind*, Scotts Valley, CA: J&C Enterprises

Grinder, J & DeLozier, J. (1987) *Turtles All The Way Down, Prerequisites to Personal Genius*, Portland, OR: Metamorphous

Grinder, J, DeLozier, J & Bandler, R. (1977) *Patterns of the Hypnotic Techniques of Milton Erickson, M.D. vol. II*, Cupertino, CA: Meta Publications

Hall, M (1996) *The Spirit of NLP*, Carmarthen, Wales: Crown House Publishing

Hall, M & Belnap, B (2004) *The Sourcebook of Magic, A comprehensive Guide to NLP Change Patterns*, Carmarthen, Wales: Crown House Publishing

Hall, M & Duval, M (2003) *Meta-Coaching: Volume II*, Clifton, CO: Neuro-Semantics

Hayes, P. (2006) *NLP Coaching*, Maidenhead: Open University Press

Holden, R. (2000) *Shift Happens; Powerful ways to transform your life, London*: Hodder Modius

Holden, R. (1998) *Happiness Now: Timeless wisdom for feeling good fast, London*: Hodder Modius

Holden, R. (2005) *Success Intelligence: Timeless wisdom for a manic society*, London: Hodder Modius

Holden, R. (2009) *Be Happy,* London: Hay House

Holden, R & Renshaw, B. (2002) *Balancing Work & Life: Essential Managers Series*, London: Dorling Kindersley

James, T & Woodsmall, W (1988) *Time Line Therapy And The Basis of Personality*, Capitola, CA: Meta Publications

Jeffers, S (1987) *Feel The Fear and Do It Anyway*, Random House Group

Knight, S (2004) *NLP at Work*, London: Nicholas Brealey

Korzybski, A (1933, 1994) *Science and Sanity: An Introduction to Non-Aristotelian Systems and General Semantics*, Lakeville, CT: The International Non-Aristotelian Library Publishing Company

Laborde, G (1987) *Influencing with Integrity, Management Skills for Communication and Negotiation*, Palo Alto, CA: Syntony

Lakoff, G. & Johnson, M. (1980) *Metaphors We Live By*, London: University of Chicago Press

Lankton, S (1980) Practical Magic, A Translation of Basic Neuro-Linguistic Programming into Clinical Psychotherapy, Carmarthen, Wales: Crown House Publishing

Lewis, B & Pucelik, F. (1990) *Magic of NLP Demystified*, Portland,Oregon: Metamorphous Press

Maupoint, M (2009) *The essential NLP practitioners handbook*, London: Live It Publishing

McMaster, M & Grinder, J (1993) *Precision : A New Approach to Communication*, Portland, OR: Metamorphous

Miller, G. (1956) *The magical number seven plus or minus two: some limits on our capacity to process information*, Psychological Review: 63; 81-97

Miller, G. A., Galanter, E. and Pribram, K. (1960) *Plans and the Structure of Behaviour*, New York: Holt Rhinehart and Winston

O'Connor, J (2001) *The NLP Workbook*, London: Element, HarperCollins

O'Connor, J & Lages, A (2004) *Coaching with NLP, How to be a Master Coach*, London: HarperCollins

O'Connor, J & Seymour, J (2002) *Introducing Neuro-Linguistic Programming*, London: HarperCollins

O'Hanlon, W (1999) *Do One Thing Different*, New York: HarperCollins

Oade, A (2009) *Starting and Running a Coaching Business*, Oxford: How To Books

Orlick, T (1998) *Embracing Your Potential*, Leeds: Human Kinetics

Orlick, T (2008) *In Pursuit of Excellence*, Leeds: Human Kinetics

Prochaska, J & DiClemente, C. (1982)*Transtheoretical therapy: Towards a more integrative model of change* Psychotherapy: Theory, Research and Practice 19 (276-88).

Renshaw, B. (2000) *Successful But Something Missing: Daring to enjoy life to the full, London*: Random House

Robbins, A. (1991) *Awaken The Giant Within*, London: Simon & Schuster

Satir, V. (1975) *Self Esteem*, Berkley, CA: Celestial Arts

Satir, V. (1976) *Making Contact*, Berkley, CA: Celestial Arts

Satir, V. (1988) *The New Peoplemaking*, Palo Alto, CA: Science and Behavior Books

Seligman, M. (2003) *Authentic Happiness*, Great Britain: Nicholas Brealey Publishing

Thomson, G & Khan, K (2008) *Magic in Practice*, London: Hammersmith Press

Whitmore, J (2002) *Coaching for Performance*, London: Nicholas Brealey

Yeager, J (1985) *Thinking about Thinking with NLP*, Cupertino CA: Meta Publications

ABOUT THE AUTHOR

Neal Anderson has over 17 years experience in developing potential and works as trainer, mentor and coach. He is the co-director of Sugar NLP based in Cumbria where he lives and runs NLP and Coach training courses and has a private coaching and psychotherapy practice.

Neal is passionate about helping people bring the best from themselves and others. He links practical experience with relevant theory to increase understanding and inspire lasting personal change. He is available for seminars and training courses throughout the country.

Neal has a Masters degree in Management from Loughborough University and is a highly skilled NLP, Coaching and Business Communications NLP Trainer (INLPTA Registered) and UKCP Registered Psychotherapist. He is a qualified Teacher (QTLS) and is an Accredited Practitioner of Outdoor Learning. His background as a Mechanical Engineer with Lucas Aerospace, Projects Manager with Sports Organisations, Heath Charities and Local Government, Outdoor Centre Director and Training Consultant gives Neal a diverse real world base from which to deliver relaxed, fun and effective training and coaching.

- For further information about certified NLP training courses visit www.sugarnlp.co.uk
- To find out more about working with Neal and coach training visit www.valleytraining.co.uk

Also from the Author
The High Performance Workbook

6 core components of excellence that build mental strength and inspire world class performance in any field. Complete with practical exercises as used by members of the UK WORLDSKILLS SQUAD and many others. 32 Pages, bound 149x210

The Fulfilling Goals Workbook

A proven 3 part programme for identifying, setting and achieving goals
If you want to achieve results, are tired of dreaming, find you never get round to making plans or want to live with real purpose then this workbook is for you. Suitable for coaches to give to their clients or to use for yourself. 36 Pages, bound 149x210

NOTES

QUICK ORDER FORM

☎ **Telephone:** (+44) 1539 737215

✉ **Email:** orders@valleytraining.co.uk

💻 **Online:** www.thenlpcoachcompanion.com

✉ **Post:** VT Publishing, 14 Sunnyside, Kendal, LA9 7DJ, UK

Please send the following books.

I understand that I may return any of them for a full refund – for any reason, no questions asked.

Title	Price	Postage	Quantity
The Fulfilling Goals Workbook	£4	£1.00	
The Fulfilling Goals Workbook Pack 10	£35	£4.50	
The High Performance Workbook	£4	£1.00	
The NLP Coach Companion	£20	£2.75	

Payment

You can order and pay online by credit card. To order by post complete the details below and send a cheque made out to Neal Anderson for the appropriate amount.

Please send more FREE information on:

❏ Speaking   ❏ Coach Training   ❏ Consultancy   ❏ Coaching

Name: _____

Address: _____

City: _____ Postcode: _____

Telephone: _____

Email address: _____